ENLIGHTENE

G000126302

RE-INTRODUCING HUMAN PRINCIPLES INTO BUSINESS

Penny Sophocleous

Published by
The Endless Bookcase Ltd.
71 Castle Road, St Albans, Hertfordshire,
England, UK, AL1 5DQ.
www.theendlessbookcase.com

First Edition
Also available in multiple e-book formats via The Endless Bookcase
website, Amazon, Nook and Kobo.

Printed in the United Kingdom
First Printing, 2016.

ISBN: 978-1-908941-57-2

ACKNOWLEDGEMENTS

Thank you to all my clients - more than a thousand of you - who chose to work with me. This book could not have been written without you. It was because I heard your thoughts, felt your feelings and understood the conflicted dynamics from your work that I came to perceive the struggles that many of you were having, trying to be enlightened leaders in an un-enlightened environment. I would like to think that this book could help bring more of us together, to make a constructive difference in the business context.

Many thanks go to William Wallace for his assistance with the research, the editing and for challenging my ideas – I have written a better book because of you. Thank you to my friends who supported me to bring this book forth, Sheila Harrison, Gail Hugman, Gill Huyton and Anne Snow. And especially to my buddy Debbie Glinnan who kept me on track, week by week, thanks! I'm grateful to Evelyn Kharag for permission to use her beautiful art on my front cover. Thanks also to family members who prefer I didn't mention them, but who were there giving me practical help, feedback and encouragement. To you all, heartfelt thanks!

REVIEW

"This is a fascinating book full of interesting anecdotes of how NOT to run a business and a model for good business. Every manager, director, VP, CEO and shareholder of all companies must read this book, take these gems on board, not just because it is the right thing to do, but because it simply makes good business sense. It provides a model for business in a future that has arrived."

Chris Moore,
Former CEO of Continental Datagraphics,
a Boeing Company

"Penny observes that the leaders of our top 1000 enterprise Corporations, hold the key to a better world. Her book Enlightened Leaders calls upon leaders everywhere to use their personal power and that of the people that comprise their organisations, to value Integrity, Trust, Truth, Respect and Fairness over pure profit. Penny sees these as the Principles that control and determine actions."

"Successful companies of the future will align the values of their Staff, their Customers and their Brand. If you are running a business and are looking for sustainable competitive advantage in a fast changing world Penny Sophocleous' book Enlightened Leaders, is a different look at leadership, that will provide your organisation with a moral compass that should line up and drive your decision making process. In a Post Volkswagen Scandal world it is a must read for decision makers everywhere."

Nick Brown,
Chairman Welwyn Hatfield Chamber of Commerce

CONTENTS

Chapter Five

Chapter Six

Chapter Twelve

ENLIGHTENED LEADERS

RE-INTRODUCING HUMAN PRINCIPLES INTO BUSINESS

INTRODUCTION

Over the last 400 years, corporations and the people who lead them seem to have gradually forgotten that the 'value to shareholders' they are all ruthlessly chasing is actually delivered by human beings, for human beings and within communities of human beings — each and every one of whom needs to be treated as such — with Truth, Respect, Trust, Justice and Integrity.

Today it seems those humane principles of Truth, Respect, Trust, Justice and Integrity are in short supply outweighed by the pursuit of money above all else. It seems that our business world has become characterised by fraud, lies, exploitation, internal corruption and failures of integrity, affecting even our premier brands (Tesco, Credit Suisse, Barclays, Volkswagen, General Motors, Royal Bank of Scotland).

This book is my contribution to redressing that balance.

In the book;

- I outline the need for a new business code.
- I propose a model for that new code, based upon five human principles of Truth, Respect, Trust, Justice and Integrity and a new alignment of Power.
- I explain each Principle and how it works when it is applied and when it isn't.
- I examine the issue of Power and how it can be re-distributed, rather than abused.
- I give a couple of examples of successful corporations who buck the trend of 'money first and foremost' to live by these human principles AND deliver increasing 'shareholder value'.
- Finally, I give some ideas on how to start to implement these principles as a leader in your own business.

> *'Altruism, generosity, solidarity and civic spirit are not like commodities that are depleted with use. They are more like ourselves that develop and grow stronger with exercise. One of the defects of a market-driven economy is that it lets these virtues languish.'*

Michael J. Sandel, in
'What Money Can't Buy'.

To renew our business life, we must exercise our human principles and their accompanying values more strongly!

Professor Sandel also says *"economics, concerned as it is with the desire for gain, does not deal with the noblest human natures"* and it is so for business. But in this book I challenge this position and ask, why not?

Why can't we have a drive for humanity and also financial gain – and in that order? Why can't we have leaders that lead for business advancement AND lead for humanity? I suggest that enlightened leaders will need to do both to create organisations that won't become obsolete; for the signs are already appearing that the rules of successful businesses are changing. New models are appearing that are demonstrating new governance structures, creating more fair and equal distributions of responsibilities, accountabilities and rewards. Leaders are invited to see better ways to lead. And if some can't yet, they can learn how to, so they can.

Enlightened Leaders

Chapter One

THE CURRENT BUSINESS CODE

How Did We Get Here?

Over the last four hundred years the corporation became a significant source of jobs and finance for people. Over that time, it has steadily encroached its power base and tentacles into people's lives, their homes, the capitalist system and markets.

The market economy and our consumer society have been built upon an ethos that puts money and profit the number one priority of all business. The pressures to deliver "value to shareholders" — ie., money, economic reporting and meeting the rules and regulations of the corporate body have overtaken whatever primary reason or purpose the organisation was first established to accomplish.

Today the majority concern and focus of conversations going on behind closed doors at Executive and Board level in global corporations (based on conversations with multiple executives of FTSE listed companies), are about costs, revenues and profit margins.

Publicly listed companies' shares are bought by shareholders who have little or nothing to do with the companies they own, other than an interest to increase their shares' value through capital appreciation or to receive ever increasing dividends. This narrow focus has concentrated a message to executive teams that they must continuously deliver ever greater revenues and profits. An alliance between shareholders and CEO's and CFO's to deliver this agenda has ensured that they have been personally well-rewarded. In conjunction with this, the rest of their work-force has had their salaries and benefits cut. The drive to return profits to shareholders has swamped the consideration of the humane needs of a company's employees, its customers and suppliers.

The legal and regulatory systems of industrialised countries have promoted the market economy and thereby the corporate economy world-wide. They have focused upon profit and the right of companies to grow and expand for their own benefit, rather than the benefits they provide to society. In particular, the US took a perverse turn in corporate development in the early 20th century. In a legal case DODGE V. FORD MOTOR COMPANY, 170 NW 668 (MICH 1919)[1] the Michigan Supreme Court held that Henry Ford owed a duty to the shareholders of the Ford Motor Company to operate his business to profit his shareholders, rather than the community as a whole or employees. Often cited as embodying the principle of "shareholder value" in companies, it became a rallying point for substantiating inhumane approaches to running businesses under the banner of maximising shareholder value.

The American corporation with its primary and exclusive focus on profit for shareholders has perverted much of the good that companies may do. It is perhaps not surprising that innovative companies such as the Valve software company have never sought external funding and are unlikely to ever float their company on an Exchange, because they do not want to lose their independence and unique culture, based on value for their employees and customers. But their example is a rarity in our world today, as entrepreneurs sell up shares in their companies to the public stock exchange in return for money and the dominance of the professional investors.

The narrowing focus for business executives in the last fifty years has been to see people as a cost to their business and an impact on their bottom line. They have dehumanised the situation in order to see people as numbers and to be able to make the case for those inanimate things to be cut from the 'company overheads'. This has translated in the economic downturn to businesses where 10 per cent of people are regularly cut from the personnel and not very much is thought about it, other than that is what is necessary to keep profits going. Some of my corporate clients over the period of 2008 - 2014 have cut 10% of their staff twice, whilst others have cut 15% or even 20% of their workforce in one process.

The industrialised nations of the world have paid a high price for their technological advancement and wealth – their humanity. The sense value for what humanity is and calls for in inter-personal relationships has been eroded substantially as the market economy and its promotion of monetary gain has become the primary goal. Various books make a compelling case for markets having taken over too much of our systems and lives, encroaching upon our personal liberty, our human equality and the promotion of corruption into every aspect of our lives, schools, hospitals, prisons, police/security, advertising and even the right of companies to buy the right to pollute our environment. (How can it ever be right for a company to buy the right to pollute our environment? Yet this is how devaluing of people's lives such a business code has become.)

The Problems the Current Code Has Caused

This narrow focus has resulted in less ethics, fewer principles, less humanity in many organisations. If humane values have appeared anywhere, they have been relegated to the Corporate Social Responsibility bracket, where echoes of the contribution that the enterprise makes into the world other than the economy, may be commented upon.

Ross McEwan, appointed chief executive of RBS in 2013 when asked by Iain Martin *"What went so badly wrong in the culture of the banks?"* said it was down to *"a single focus on profitability... an ever increasing desire to improve profit results year on year to give back to shareholders."* Iain Martin, * *'Making it Happen: Fred Goodwin, RBS and the Men who blew Up the British Economy'*. p. 291

The bailouts of the banks, the Eurozone sovereign debt crisis, plus all the other financial dislocations, recessions, market rigging, widespread fraud and widening gaps between the rich and the poor all around the world, may come to be recognised as the ultimate results of such a focus.

The current business code has caused corporations to become sick by their focus on only one thing. For over eight years now, we have suffered the outcomes of a malaise that has been generated by people who have focused too much on money and very little else. It has caused toxicity in our world-wide systems that cannot be fixed or made well by anything within the economic system. Agritech companies that promote genetically mutated seeds that prevent Indian farmers from generating their own seeds, is one major example of companies whose focus on the bottom line causes widespread problems for others that they take no accountability for.

Many clients of banks and utility companies feel exploited by their actions, which has resulted in costs being borne not by them, but by people who are their customers (and everyone else in the land) who have no power to say 'No'. People living in countries where mining and oil companies are extracting their land's natural resources feel exploited because such contracts go to make a few people very rich, whilst the rest are impacted very little in terms of benefits or improvements.

Executives choose not to take account of the human beings that will be affected by their decisions and choose instead to harden their hearts and focus on numbers that cannot speak back to them.

Should it not be a requirement upon leaders to think about more than just the bottom line?

The world's central banks' adoption of "quantitative easing" that aimed to avoid the negative impacts of recession, have not stopped them and recessions have happened anyway. The other solutions to be re-introduced, including new rules of conduct and regulatory frameworks are still embedded in the financial and economic focus that are likely to cause the system to fail again.

Exploitation of Employees

Large corporations today use their employees as the mechanism to deliver the business activities in the same way as machines were used in the Industrial Revolution — used for the least amounts of money that they can be accessed for and then discarded if their costs become too high. In the same way as technology is replaced with new, higher specifications and more efficiency, workers in some countries are now disposed of so their work can be transferred to workers living in more deprived circumstances, in poorer nations. Outsourcing is the catch-word to describe the betrayal and lack of loyalty of companies to their employees.

We like to think we have progressed significantly as a society (and perhaps for some of us in the highly developed world we have). But the developed world is exporting its practises of exploitation to poor countries and using people like machines; where corporations can now pay wages of 2 dollars a day to workers rather than employing a person in their home country to do the same job that would cost 90 dollars a day. When I have challenged executives about such practises, they emphasise that their organisation is spreading its riches around the world by providing employment; with salaries that are fair in the local community and which are raising people out of poverty.

Before industrialisation, we didn't know how to use people as machines – though feudalism and indentured service often used people as workers in an inhumane way. Slavery has been rife in different ages and different communities and even today, indentured servants and workers in some countries are treated in ways that are very close to slavery. In fact, the needs of servicing the West's retailers often call for people to be brought from other countries or parts of their own country, into cities where they have no homes and are reliant upon their employer for residential facilities. Victims of trafficking for forced labour lose their freedom, becoming modern-day slaves. Human trafficking represented an estimated $31.6 billion of international trade per annum in 2010 (which may be part of the side effects of global corporation practices). It is estimated that 22 million people today still live and work in slavery.

By looking around our world we can see many instances of exploitation – perpetrated by globalisation and corporations who have little concern for anything but profit. People trafficking are occurring as a part of the process of industrial production (though global corporations seek to distance themselves from such practises). Personal freedoms are being restricted (especially of women or minority cultures) and if you are living in a poor country, corporate entities are invited (often by your government) to come and exploit you, in near similar conditions as they exploited workers in newly industrialised Britain two centuries ago. How many people are working or living in exploitative, unhealthy conditions has not been counted, but it could be anywhere between several hundred million and a billion people.

Inequality of Benefits and Salaries

The view that businesses are there to provide a service or product that serves humanity, clashes with the reality of how many businesses go on and what in truth they do. The concentration of power into the Executive Board has meant that that power has been abused and salaries and benefits have been awarded unequally to those at the top. The directors of many publicly quoted businesses appear to use the business that they run primarily to serve them personally, their cronies secondly, shareholders thirdly, while serving humanity comes later in priority.

The balances of power have been shaken and placed into too few hands, hands that too many times use the power to benefit themselves and deny the rights of others. Media stories of cut-backs where this led to lower salaries for the highest paid were few and far between, though lower salaries for the lowly paid workers were regularly reported. In the stock market, a company's share price will rise on the announcement of job cuts, because it is widely recognised that less people doing all the jobs will lead to more profits.

Today we are in a situation where politics and laws set the benchmarks for what is good practice and companies are then required to meet those requirements. But political systems are running well behind the developments that have occurred in our market economy and do not address the inequalities and abuse that have become the norm in business.

Corporate Hardheartedness and Impact On Human Health

To reiterate, business often dehumanises the humans that work for it, the customers which it serves, the suppliers who support it, and the shareholders who fund it. It does this with labels, by the focus on what all of these people 'DO' for the business, rather than who they are and by clumping them all together as a group and addressing them as that group. Annual reports are classically where readers can see the extent of the dehumanisation that has taken place in the Board and company. Its reports demonstrate how far leaders have separated themselves out from the people involved in the day to day, human to human interaction that is the reality of people doing business.

Such hardheartedness has become an ingrained cultural print that characterises some organisations in many of our world's capitals, especially in London, New York, Tokyo, Hong Kong, Singapore and Beijing. Employee suicides or death from overwork are not monitored in the UK, but they are now in Japan. Today more than 2000 applications for workers' compensation or survivors' benefits are filed annually by workers or families seeking state recognition for death, disability or depression caused by overwork. Experts say these claims are just the tip of the iceberg: as many as 8000 of Japan's roughly 30,000 annual suicides are thought to be work-related. Experts say that the true toll is probably much higher, since 10 per cent of the male labour force work 60-plus-hour weeks under the same conditions as those who die or become mentally unstable. It is estimated that there are more than 10,000 non-suicide *karoshi* deaths each year, recognising the part that accumulated fatigue has in causing certain kinds of cardiovascular disease.

It has become very clear that the absence of human principles in business leads to a variety of illnesses, stresses, anxieties and serious injury, of an emotional and mental kind. It is shocking, in particular since 2008 and the financial crash, that the amount of pressure and inhumane responses that people have been subject to by a mechanistic, 'achievement focused environment' has been huge. People have encountered mental and emotional pressure that required them to behave like machines and to ignore their real human feelings. Mass redundancies created 'survivor syndrome' – where people left in work are discouraged from speaking about those who left or acknowledging their own feelings about the redundancies — until they themselves fall ill and have to take time off. Another trend in big business is where a person commits suicide (sometimes because of extreme pressure at work) and everyone else has to just 'get on with it', without being offered counselling or help to deal with their grief.

Businesses are creating mental illnesses in their employees which they don't recognise or acknowledge, often attributing it to individual weakness or poor performance. In my experience, this has particularly affected the consulting professions, the legal and accountancy firms whose businesses rely upon the delivery of services by experts in their field. Generating fees in some high performance environments have on occasion led to pressure on people to work long hours –

often well in excess of their statutory hours. Where this has become the norm (and this may be generous), in at least 10% of international law firms, 50 to 75 hours per week is normal. Maintained over years, such hard work builds into burnout. Stress and illness are early symptoms which some employers prefer to ignore and when employees can't hack it any more, they are happy to pay off the individual, using the excuse of redundancy or compromise agreements to remove them from the company.

Big business's focus on solely economic factors has made our places of work sick with pressure, stress and resentments. It is based on a misunderstanding of human beings and their interest or purpose in working and a belief that money and benefits are all that they seek. The human pain and suffering of such cuts are often ignored as people are led to believe that it's a clear choice between cutting staff or the organisation not being able to survive.

If I identify the failings of our economic system and multi-national companies with their resulting ramifications, in small, I see the same failures occurring in smaller business organisations. These failures may not impact billions of people but they impact hundreds and thousands of people working in small to medium size companies. The same failures of integrity, respect, truth, and justice have as many fall-outs impacting individuals and teams as larger groups in international companies. These failures of humanity result in stress, anxieties, serious injury to mental and emotional well-being and breakdown in careers, even to suicides and death.

This unhealthy trend should not be allowed to continue or be promulgated to other parts of the world. To counteract this trend, I offer a framework for thinking through the introduction of principles into business that recognises the value of people and requires a re-prioritising of the thinking and systems of business.

Environments That Make People Sick

Organisations need to address the environmental factors inside the people who work for them as well as the external. There are professionals who conduct environmental health audits, but toxic relationships are not on the audit checklist. Cultures of blame or bullying have as much power to hurt people as redundancies. The health and wellbeing of employees should be the concern of leaders, not the remit of a few HR professionals whose views can be easily disrespected and discounted. The closest thing that most organisations use is the Engagement Survey and what is this measuring? How committed and engaged its people feel, so that they might continue to be employed, rather than disclosing their well-being or happiness.

Were someone to conduct a health audit on our working culture, they might be asking the following:

- Does the work we ask people to do allow them to be in their parasympathetic system rather than their sympathetic system?
- How much of people's time at work is in a 'fight or flight' response? ie., stress?

- If people's activities are generating a stress response, ie., causing their limbic system to trigger, leading to a fight or flight response, are we causing illness in that person?
- How many executives' or managers' normal days consist of running on adrenalin all day?
- Does our business make people sick or well?

Stress responses cause illness, whilst operating in a relaxed mode allows the body to engage in natural healing and generates feelings of well-being. Too many times, leaders in organisations create a culture that actually makes people ill. Various instances in my experience demonstrate this.

Whilst working with an individual in the financial services sector, the person exhibited ongoing stress behaviours. They often mentioned how stressful the working environment was, particularly as two of the senior Executives were at war with each other which cascaded down into competitive, antagonistic behaviours between their team members. At another organisation, one of their employees collapsed with a heart attack and died. He had been at work for twenty-four hours. Such behaviours are not untypical in IT projects with deadlines to meet, or during IPO preparations in the finance sector or M & A transactions in the legal sector.

Employees' resignation from their companies over such stressful experiences and environments are often dismissed with disrespectful comments about their weakness of character and incompetence. Such reactions defend an unhealthy environment and ensure that leaders' blind spots continue to be in place. For the individual leaving the company however, this doesn't always result in a speedy return to well-being; such experiences often leave huge shocks in the employee's physical, mental and emotional systems that may take several years to get over. Such occurrences should be a wake-up call to leaders in organisations that they need to effect serious change.

In another instance, a senior executive had extreme stress patterns in his conversations, behaviours and style of interactions. Over lunch one day, I jokingly asked him to calm down a little, as his style of communication was such as to make me feel very nervous and concerned that he might have a heart attack. He and many other leaders can't recognise what relaxed working looks like and take being hyped up with adrenalin constantly as the norm. In some cultures, unless executives can boast of being really busy and be seen to be rushing about from one meeting to the next and have to work late into the night, it is suggested that they are not working hard enough.

Such egotistically driven behaviour is mentally unhealthy and should be called out as such, but who has the guts and courage to call it in their work environment? It is egotism of the worst sort — self-deluded aggrandisement — based on what they want others to think about them, rather than be concerned with the truth. Such people will in all likelihood not know how wrong they are until and if, they hurt themselves or others through pressure and overwork. One global company's experience resulted in their CFO committing suicide (in part) due to pressure from the

Chairman of the company. The Chairman resigned immediately when this news hit the worldwide press.

Other examples come to mind. When people suffering from stress try to return to work, they are often assisted by people with no formal training on how to help them return to the normal pressures and strains of their work environment. Some senior executives are asked to support people returning after mental health issues (brought on by burnout, stress and over-exertion in the company) to help them acclimatise to work in a less stressful way and to slowly get used to working again. But they are not given any advice on how to help them, having to resort to their own humanity to deal with them; which is ironic and demonstrates how little humanity is considered at higher levels of the organisation.

Corporate Criminality and the Breakdown Of Ethics

Corporate criminality has been increasing since the 1980's. A listing of the *'Top 100 Corporate Criminals of the Decade'* was compiled by Russell Mokhiber, using the conservative definition of 'corporations that have pled guilty or no contest to crimes and have been criminally fined'. His list of corporate criminals identifies criminals in the 1990's and falls into 14 categories of crime: Environmental (38), antitrust (20), fraud (13), campaign finance (7), food and drug (6), financial crimes (4), false statements (3), illegal exports (3), illegal boycott (1), worker death (1), bribery (1), obstruction of justice (1) public corruption (1), and tax evasion (1).

> *"The list of the top hundred corporate criminals of the 1990's delivers a few messages. One is the breadth of corporate crime and how many different corporations, including many of the leading corporations in the country and in the world, are involved in criminal activities. There's pervasiveness to corporate criminality. It tells us though, how small the fines were for most of the companies involved. Fines on the order of a million dollars may mean something to an individual but to a large multinational corporation, a million dollars is something to be laughed off. It's very little sanction and no deterrent really, whatsoever."*

What the List Tells Us,
Robert Weissman, Editor, Multinational Monitor*

Breakdowns of trust have occurred when news of corporate criminality has become public (sometimes well after such criminals have severely damaged people, their wealth or the environment). Enron, WorldCom, Arthur Anderson, BCCI, LTCM and Madoff Investment Securities LLC are the ones with the greatest impact. Were anyone to compile such a list for the last 10 years we might see many more, including Volkswagen, a formerly trusted brand and many more in the finance section!

During the last decade there have been many instances of corrupt and fraudulent practises involving market rigging, insider trading and collusion in banks and other industries across the world. Such examples demonstrate the inherent lack of integrity woven into the fabric of how things are done in some industries and the resulting breakdowns of trust.

Since 2008, the U.S. authorities have imposed fines of over $100bn on its largest banks. The FSA in the UK set fines of over £835.5 million in the 10 years between 2003 and 2013, whilst in 2014, the FCA instituted fines of £1.47 billion. In a speech, Tracey McDermott, Director of Enforcement and Financial Crime at the Financial Conduct Authority, said "So, trust is not only critical but the cost of getting it wrong is very clear."* Altogether, these fines represent a colossal failure on the part of our political leaders, regulators, law-enforcement officials and bankers. What are we to make of a system that allows individuals to ignore fundamental honesty and truth, blatantly violate regulations and laws that govern their organisation's existence and flagrantly benefit themselves in the process? Or, that there have been no sanctions exercised over any of the individuals who have done this, no public shaming, no penalties such as being sent to jail?

These collective results suggest that lack of integrity has become part of the system of business and that, quite rightly, we should not trust business. Fining the organisation penalizes shareholders, not the traders, managers or executives who execute or permit the fraud. This puts all of us in danger of enabling "gangsters" to run our institutions – both banks and regulators — who will not take on the legal challenge required to bring to justice, not the institutions, but the individuals who have perpetuated criminal activities within the society we all inhabit. Matt Taibbi writing about these issues titles his article *'Gangster Bankers: Too Big to Jail*** and says the United States by not prosecuting HSBC for its many failures of non compliance with US laws was itself *"slipping toward a third-world-nation status of dubious legal protections and the worst form of cronyism."* The cost of committing crimes should be more than an expensive fine paid by someone else. It should involve jail time. We risk far too much otherwise.

As the latest economic fall-out was precipitated by a breakdown of integrity, it has caused many people to consider how to ensure it doesn't happen again.

SUMMARY

In our twenty-first century world, the kings that rule our world are not monarchs, they are the senior executives that run the trans-national organisations that are the biggest 1000 corporations in the world; that generate revenues and profits that well exceed the national GDP of many of the poorest nations of our planet. It is to them, as well as all the business owners and entrepreneurs that are building our future's significant businesses, that my book is addressed. For who among them stops to consider the temporal power they wield and what mercy should be in their hearts when making decisions that affect those that work for them, those that supply them and the customers who buy products from them?

By changing the principles at the heart of our businesses, we shall be able to change the content of the conversations we have, to make our environments at work healthier, mentally, emotionally and financially.

It is time to overwrite old human responses to abuse or corruption, such as revenge and operating by the letter of the law and in Shakespeare's words come from a new perspective:

> Portia: *The quality of mercy is not strained;*
> *It droppeth as the gentle rain from heaven*
> *Upon the place beneath. It is twice blest:*

It blesseth him that gives, and him that takes

It is time to recognise that our world calls for more enlightened leaders, that understand that principles and ethics need to be the touchstone of their everyday decision making; that they are responsible for role-modelling behaviours that require Truth, Respect, Justice and Fairness, Integrity and Trust to be the standard for all employee behaviours; Enlightened leaders who understand that the old paradigm of hierarchical companies may be coming to an end and that their organisation may become obsolete without the innovative creativity that can come from all of their employees, their customers and their suppliers contributing their trust to its survival.

Chapter Two

A NEW BUSINESS CODE IS REQUIRED

The economic crisis, bailouts, unemployment, cutbacks and resulting recessions around the world since 2008 were not a failure caused by economics; they were a failure of people's humanity.

They denote the absence of Integrity, Respect, Truth, Trust and Justice in the hearts of the people who caused the problems and of those who created the 'solutions'.

They are the result of the inhumanity of those who fed their greed, perpetuated corruption, exercised their weakness and actively disrespected and abused their customers, colleagues and shareholders.

They are the result of the lack of insight of those in power who are unable to see alternatives to its continuance or to show a moral or ethical way forward — whose responses are at best pragmatic and at worst, morally reprehensible.

Where corrections are to be made, they need to happen in the fibres of people's humanity.

A new business code is called for. A new business code that answers the question 'What truly will make work effective, in healthy environments that will enable people to thrive?'

Seeing The Problem

The problem is caused by the current 'code' dominating business ie., making money comes first – expressed as the duty of a business to promote only 'shareholder value'.

At present, the Code that most businesses operate is to make the most amount of money, with the least amount of costs, to deliver products and services that people will buy. For most of my life, this made sense. I no longer believe that that is enough. We must ask more of ourselves, to serve a higher purpose than merely adding to a consumer society that grows by consuming more, using up more of the planet's resources each year and polluting our environments and lives with so much 'stuff'.

Businesses were originally created to provide a service or product that serves humanity. The original purpose for an organisation's existence is often forgotten and making ever more money in order to continue to benefit its executives and shareholders, overtake the original purpose and the benefits that it was originally established to deliver. Businesses need to reconnect to the purposes for which they were created and for which they exist. It is understood that a business cannot continue to exist unless it remains economically viable, but its profitability should not be the sole or most important focus.

To correct this distortion, business needs to insert into all its structures, fundamental principles that take account of the human beings that operate in it, the human beings that it serves and the human beings that supply it or are impacted by it, in its local communities.

We need a business code that balances making money with enabling people to express their innate talents; that delivers service and value to its customers while making reasonable profits; that serves a useful purpose in the world, whilst not damaging our planet's environment. We need a business code that re-prioritises an organisation's value for people and their place in its business and defocuses upon making its executives rich and powerful. We need a business code that contributes to all of its peoples' (employees, customers and suppliers) well-being and sense of rightness.

Ha-Joon Chang in his book '23 *Things They Don't Tell You About Capitalism** quotes a Kobe steel manager slapping down a bunch of economists for their ignorance about how business really works. He paraphrases the manager *"our board of directors routinely approves the majority of projects submitted by our employees, because we believe that our employees work for the good of the company. ...You simply cannot run a large bureaucratic organisation, be it Kobe Steel or your government, if you assume that everyone is out for himself."* The author, being an economist, humbly reflects that he found it a *"powerful testimony to the limitations of standard economic theory, which assumes that self-interest is the only human motivation that counts."*

A new business code needs to facilitate the generosity of the spirit of people, enabling their talents to be expressed; where people are allowed to express their value and be recompensed appropriately for it. If we could envision a world where all countries were similarly rich, poverty was eliminated and we all had a good standard of living and people were similarly compensated, would not the Code under which we did business be different?

In nations and local communities such as Bhutan or Bali, where industrialisation and capitalisation have not yet been introduced as a major focus of human activity, humane motivations and interactions still have sway and are the well-spring of behaviour and trade.

We need to ask more of business people in the developed world. We need to ask our leaders and companies to act in accordance with principles that support the expansion of humanity in our world. We need to have different conversations in business, not just about performance, profits, or quarterly or annual results, but rather the principles that make humans thrive. Conversations need to be had around an organisation's purpose, meaning, significance, contribution and generation of value to all stakeholders. They need to be about an individual's contribution and participation in the purpose, contribution to the enterprise, as well as their personal growth and development, because the organisations which have such conversations will survive and grow, whereas those who don't, won't.

Corporate Social Responsibility is often referred to as a new Business Code that organisations can look to for advice on how they can make a positive difference to their community. CSR requires organisations to benefit the local communities in which they work, but there are wide differences of understanding about what this means. Integrated Reporting is a more recent agenda that asks companies to report on a wider number of issues, but does not include values or principles or humane matters within it. The same thing with sustainability – it's an issue that has been taken up by some businesses taking steps to minimise their environmental impact – which is good, but all of these initiatives have resulted in fragmented and inconsistent mindsets and organisational behaviours.

The devastating effects of climate change and global warming are the burning platform upon which we all live and this should be generating a powerful noise that gets all of our attention; it demands that we see the world differently and that we operate in a different way. It calls for all of us to re-assess what we call useful work that is valuable for us as people? Is it valuable work that doesn't harm us or our environment?

It appears that most people in business have now to re-learn what principles need to be brought into the workplace and what impact that will have on our humanity. Some aspects relating to greed and unethical behaviours that have arisen in the business community have been formalised into law respecting governance, compliance, anti-bribery and corruption. The other initiatives that have been volunteered by companies have been to formalise a set of values that executives promote to their employees as guideposts for looked-for behaviours. However, many executives are now cynical of these 'so-called values' because they're often there for show, and not for non-negotiable standards of behaviours that are required of everyone (with penalties for non-compliance). Values are often fuzzy 'nice to haves' but ignored when advantage can be had by behaving in ways that are not aligned to those values, when they would be costly to the organisation.

Most organisations put profits in front of people, both employees and customers and the few organisations who choose not to do that, stand out as unusual examples. An organisation's primary mission should be to benefit all human beings that choose to be involved with it, whether employees, customers, shareholders, third parties and direct suppliers; and that it should do no harm to any of the environments in which it operates.

There are some organisations that show us a different way forward and I have many examples of them in future chapters. This first one demonstrates most vividly what can happen in an organisation when its leaders choose to make their values non-negotiable and act from them like principles.

Case Study

Norton Rose Fulbright (a law firm in the UK) when confronted with the economic downturn in 2008 chose a different way. Their partners chose not to compromise their integrity or their principles.

They determined to find a way which would allow them to retain all their employees, who they saw as their community. They heard of a programme that KPMG was introducing and took pains to understand the details of it and devised something similar for their organisation. The programme entailed two elements –

a staff reduction of the working week, from five to four days, with a reduction to 85% of salary — and an offer to anyone who wished to take a sabbatical of between 4 to 6 weeks, at 30% of salary. They called their programme Flex, and they asked all partners to sign up first, then they consulted with 2,000 employees in the UK. They had forecast that they needed 75% buy in to the proposal. They achieved 96%, 11,000 employees in total!

They saw this as a fantastic achievement which meant that they did not have to make anyone redundant and would allow them to respond in an agile way to client demands and developments in the market. This strategy demonstrated the integrity of their brand, as an employer of choice for employees, enabling them to retain staff longer and as an employer of choice for new employees. The commercial impact was highly favourable too. It meant that they saved themselves the costs of paying redundancies and the costs of re-hiring people, when market conditions improved. A further result was three clients of the firm hearing of their programme called and wanted to know more. All three on hearing details chose to implement something very similar in their organisation.

The partners of Norton Rose demonstrated high levels of enlightened leadership, firstly by choosing to stand by their principles and maintain their integrity and secondly through the implementation phase which required a great deal of respectful attention and management. They formed a very senior business team to manage the programme, liaise with partners in different groups regarding their resourcing needs, set up an intranet site for Q&A's and other information for staff, and developed an online calendar to oversee requirements. At all times, the execution process demonstrated their integrity and respect for their people. Some support staff could not manage a drop to a four-day week and mostly their need to work full-time was respected. Whereas some lawyers saw this as a great opportunity to take a sabbatical, and many were facilitated to take time out to refresh themselves through rest, travel or undertaking different activities.

The Flex programme was initiated on 1 May 2009 and ended in January 2010.

When asked what the organisation has learnt as a result, Lak Purewal, the Head of HR said that they had learnt:

1. Don't follow the crowd.
2. The programme enabled them to be more creative.
3. Flexible working can work, but it means putting in systems and processes that facilitate it.
4. They saw the value of concerted, committed action. The programme needed the majority of people to make it work and they saw how valuable partners and employees commitment to the same things could be.
5. They saw that they had acted in accordance with their principles, Quality, Unity, Integrity and this was deeply satisfying.

The longer term impact for Norton Rose was that in the three years afterwards, there was very good engagement of people, with a 'feel-good factor' that characterized relationships and interactions. The high value that they said they had for people had been demonstrated and lived. The trust that had been built into relationships had not been betrayed. Taking the humane approach did not lead to failure or uneconomic results. In fact, Lak Purewal, the Head of HR told me that the outcomes were highly positive, leading to high levels of retention (of employees and clients) that led to extremely positive economic results in subsequent years.

This example and a few others demonstrate that putting people before profits can lead to highly positive outcomes, economic as well as some which cannot be measured. What price can be put on maintaining integrity for each and every one of the partners who lived through this experience? What price can be put on not betraying trust? How can the 'feel-good factors' that each employee of Norton Rose at the time and afterwards had, be measured in hard numbers? They can't.

What if we were to value our human experience first, and considered that feeling good was of primary importance to each of us? We might act with that in mind and give ourselves and others better experiences as a first consideration and better salaries as second. It's as John Lennon said *"When I went to school, they asked me what I wanted to be when I grew up. I wrote down 'happy'. They told me I didn't understand the assignment, and I told them they didn't understand life"*.

When you act in accordance with principles that you have determined thoughtfully and through deep consideration this will bring happiness and ease. If one third of your life (at least) is spent at work and you're not able to live in integrity with your principles, this will lead to unhappiness and 'dis-ease'. Such issues are not normally spoken of within the context of business. Success is only related to power, position, money and peripheral economic benefits; but this invalidates the most important part of human lives, our feelings, sense of spirit and connection to personal purpose and wish for contribution. Yet another positive example is Tony

Hsieh, CEO of Zappos.com, Inc. a shoe company based in the US, who has made 'Delivering Happiness' his company's mission and has built a phenomenally successful and happy organisation. *

Enlightened Future Perspectives

It is possible in 100 years in the future, when people look back to our time, at the prevailing business attitudes, practises and behaviours that they will think about us in the same way as we think about the 18th century and the practices of early industrialisation and slavery. They will be able to look at today and see evidence of the exploitation of the weak by corporate entities and the enforcement of corporate rights over the human rights of individuals.

Businesses underestimate the value systems that make people buy one thing over another, or shop in one store over another. Yes, in a world where poverty is the predominant experiential factor in peoples' lives, they will choose stores and products that are the cheapest; but if poverty wasn't driving every choice, then people would and do, use different factors to determine who and where they will interact to buy their goods.

Today we can see that where people are not subject to the restraint of poverty, they do choose differently and choose very much more on experiential and value based reasons. If we think about the John Lewis Partnership, (a retail chain based in the UK) most everything about the organisation is different and is responded to differently by its customers. Its standard 'Never knowingly undersold' means that they will sell you a product at the same price as is being sold by any other organisation (including if on sale elsewhere), has created a committed loyal customer base. The organisation is employee owned and all of their staff owns a share of the company. Its customers appreciate being served by people who respect themselves and their customer, who are joint owners of the business and are proud of their company. Customers appreciate that they take ownership of the environment in which they work and deal with their customers in a friendly, respectful manner and where their suppliers are respected and dealt with in a manner that makes them partners to the Partnership.

Customers may not always be aware of the Principled and rule-based systems that sit at the heart of the operation of the John Lewis Partnership. Their principles and rules are not advertised. However, it is those principles and rules that make all the difference in determining attitudes, behaviours and organisational responses that build trust, a certainty and confidence in their customers, their suppliers and their stakeholders/local communities. Their example is rare against many other corporate environments which do not uphold value systems or a business code that supports the people who work for them, the suppliers who support them, or the customers who buy from them.

Chapter Three

OUR COMMON AND EVOLVING HUMAN CONSCIOUSNESS

This book is for those leaders in business who have recognised some or all of the things that I recognise, who think they're the only ones. So many of you feel you're on your own — that those around you in your business don't recognise the value of these perceptions. This is a rallying point to those enlightened leaders who want to act to make a change in the culture of your business but can't see how. Who feel they can't do it on their own.

This book attempts to help people and companies think through how to get ahead of the curve, to help them define what excellent practices, rules, standards and behaviours would look like from the human standpoint; and to help their leaders role model the mindsets, the attitudes and behaviours that belong with a humane framework and mindset. It is for business leaders who truly want to lead with new thought and new perceptions, who recognise that by growing their own consciousness of what is right and decent for them, they can perceive better ways to improve the working life of their employees and stakeholders. That by putting people first, they can recruit the natural creativity and innovation of all people to develop much better solutions for the challenges facing us all.

There are already some organisations who demonstrate the validity and good business outcomes that result from people doing the humane thing. When human beings do the right thing, there are many satisfactions that are their own reward that cannot be measured by money, though they may be measured by reputational credibility, customer satisfactions, sharing wealth and purpose, long-term legitimacy and legacy.

If we consider human evolution at the business level, we are at a point where we are seeing new trends of behaviours (coming from new technology and innovation) that will move business and the way it deals with its people into new values and behaviours. Some radical new thinking is required. As humans we already have a variety of frameworks that could, if we approach the business environment with an evolved view, help us deal with our current and some of our long standing problems more easily.

As Einstein suggested, the problem of a thing cannot be solved by looking for a solution in the same area that caused it. Solutions for breakdowns in integrity, trust, abuse of power will not be found in our economic systems. We need to look at the people that work in our businesses, especially the leaders who exercise the most power, for ways that would allow for a new direction to be set inside organisations, for its people, suppliers and its customers.

We need to examine those humane principles that are natural, that make us work well as a specie, as well as individuals within groups; we are all subject to the innate nature of humanity however the cultural differences between us appear to divide us. The principles which are innate in all human beings derive out of our core natures, so they are really meant for all human beings, not just for those inhabiting Western liberal culture. Few people go to school to learn about humanity but we experience it all the same. We go to school to learn our language, history and maths, but not to learn about feeling valued, or about respect or truth, for these things are known when they are experienced.

The language of humanity is universal. All humans share it, whatever race, colour or creed, and it is the language of emotions. All humans experience feelings and emotions in similar ways and they feel love, anger, care, fear, compassion in similar ways. Feelings cannot be coloured by the judgemental bias of the mind and we don't need a dictionary to understand the feelings of people impacted in positive or negative ways by their work. Yet it is people's feelings that can become the most damaged by corrupt or wrongly focused practises at work.

Leaders need to understand deeper truths of what makes human beings work well and even themselves. They need to understand people; not just how to manipulate them to perform, but to meet their needs and create a contract of equality, where they are not taken advantage of but are recompensed fairly for their contribution. My mission is to generate different types of conversation in business, not around performance or the bottom line, profits, revenues or quarterly or annual results, but rather the principles that make humans thrive.

In recent years Values have been promoted as inspirational mindsets for leaders to adopt. However, such values have not translated into required standards or norms that are expected of all people throughout the organisation. This has resulted in Values being displayed in Annual Reports, or on the wall at Head Office, but rarely has a penalty been exercised for people not behaving in accordance with those values. Values generally do not call for rules to be created around them, enabling people to claim their interpretation of that value and what it might call for in behaviours is correct. There isn't the clear-cut clarity that comes from stating something is a Principle that has rules, penalties and standards delineated against it that people are required to meet. People are rarely held to account for their Values; but they may be for Principles clearly clarified and stated against required standards of behaviours and organisational response.

This book asks for more than introducing humane values into the workplace; it makes a distinction between Values and Principles. It highlights that values mostly mean an ideal intangible that is aspired to, as an attitude, an internal feeling for some higher quality of expression that is sought after and influences behaviour. Values are abstract concepts of what is important and worthwhile, and represent broad preferences concerning appropriate courses of action or outcomes. Values are subjective and vary across individuals and cultures, and are in many ways aligned with beliefs and belief systems that may or may not support certain standards or behaviours.

A Principle however, relates to a law or rule that makes things work a particular way. Its starting point is that as a human race – our common 'Humanity' — issues from a Principle that generates laws and rules that are valid for all people. We are much more likely to find in Principles a greater clarity that enables us to operate more naturally and beneficially.

This book is an exposition of those principles that make us a properly operating human system that naturally and easily generates our humanity. The principles are unlikely to surprise, as they are features of our every-day life and are referred sometimes as standards of what we would like to see or express. The mundane and the important are distinguished and positioned differently from how perhaps they have been previously considered.

My starting point is that despite all the business, cultural, religious, ethical and political differences between people, despite the various indoctrinations we have each been subject to, we are human beings with the same body and systems that think act and feel in the same way. So whether we're Indian, Chinese, American, African, Japanese, English, Egyptian or Italian, our fundamental feelings are the same. And whatever business or industry we work in the same human issues confront us.

We share the same innate intelligence and the same emotional equipment that enables us to respond in very similar ways. We know when humanity is at play and when it is not. There is in all of us an innate measuring system that comes with birth and is developed through the normal process of growing up. Human feelings are already in our constitution and operate in us whether we're thinking about them or not, in the same way that our heart beats and our digestive system works without our interference.

This has created a collective consciousness and awareness which is continuously evolving. As our human consciousness has evolved, we need a clearer and more meaningful purpose for what we do, that is greater than making money. This influences all of us, not just the Gen Y generation, who are its greatest exponent.

Outstanding enlightened leaders such as Nelson Mandela, by their life and behaviour show us a better way. The establishment of Truth and Reconciliation Commission introduced a new standard for neutralising conflicts. It was an innovative model for building peace and justice and for holding accountable those guilty of human rights violations, whilst laying the foundation for building reconciliation among all South Africans. This innovation – to provide amnesty to those asking for it as part of their truth-speaking – helped heal the country and bring about a reconciliation of its people. Its emphasis was on gathering evidence and uncovering information—from both victims and perpetrators—and not on prosecuting individuals for past crimes and differed vastly from the Nuremberg trials that prosecuted Nazis after World War II. As a result of such leadership many other countries dealing with post-conflict issues have instituted similar methodologies for such commissions.

Nelson Mandela was only able to come to such innovative and enlightened responses to apartheid, because of his own evolved consciousness. He speaks in his biography *'Long Walk to Freedom'* of how his 27 years' imprisonment allowed him the reflection time to realise how forgiveness and reconciliation were better antidotes to the past than revenge. His countrymen and women were able to leave behind the injustices of the past and progress to a better future, by adopting the need for Truth without punishment, enabling forgiveness and reconciliation.

In the business context, if leaders would engage with human beings in their business, whether customers, employees, or suppliers from the perspective detailed above, they would derive better answers to the challenges that face them. They would create not only more profitable businesses, but a better world for all human beings. By coming into deeper insights into people and their needs, we would create more enlightened leaders that would deliver humane cultures and purpose-aligned businesses that meet people's need to contribute whilst not damaging them.

There is an inherent value to principle based businesses, ones that align to the humane nature of people; which have empathy for their right to work that provides them interest, reward and satisfaction; one that leads them to the acquiring of happiness and well-being. There are already some businesses established on a principled basis, which have conscious aims of the kind I mention here; businesses that do not put profit first, but third or fourth in priority. These companies are successful!

Enlightened Leaders

Chapter Four

THE HUMANITY PRINCIPLES MODEL

Humanity – A Definition

Humanity means to think of and to treat people as human beings with feelings, awareness and sensitivities that make them unique and individual with a life and purpose that is their own; not as objects, or machines that are there to be used for other people's purposes. Human beings have life, consciousness, feelings, standing, capability and stature in the world with each person being entitled to the same human rights and being treated as having equal worth and value. Each person's expression, way and style and output may be different and may vary depending on their uniqueness, as well as their environment, opportunity and education.

Humanity in this context relates to the best parts of our consciousness. These humane aspects reflect the best kind of thinking and feeling that come from our mental, emotional and spiritual constitution. Much of our physical environment has been changed to construct layers of structure, order, cleanliness and functionality inside of which we live. Through technology, many parts of our world have people living lifestyles today that were previously only accessed by kings and queens.

The external changes that have occurred over the millennia in our housing, material goods and technology are easy to see, but have there also been internal changes that makes us better today than once we were? If any, such changes are housed in the neural pathways of our brains and mind and the ethical alignments that we have disseminated across the planet through our nations, cultures, religions and global communications processes. Such changes at brain level act to control some of the lower standards of reactions that our local cultural filters may have given us; eg., Greeks traditionally reacted in a racist manner to Turkish people, but with some effort, any such programming can be overcome and not responded to.

An instance of this was when the Chinese authorities opened fire upon protestors in the Tiananmen Square protests of 1989 and then had to confront the world's outrage; similarly, in America when police have fired upon black people and people died. External pressures like these lead to subtle and progressive changes in the national psyche, changing people's views on which behaviours are acceptable going forward and which are not. Racial inequality in America resulted in the African-American Civil Rights Movement in the 50's and 60's with Martin Luther King's campaign for equal treatment under the law.

Our times are struggling with the same issues that the Greeks and the Romans struggled with in their societies two thousand years ago. Many nations, both in the West and in India, China and South America are experiencing the same problems of power and the dominance by the few over the many. Joseph E. Stiglitz in *'The Price of Inequality'* provides a penetrating insight into America's journey into the widening gap of economic and political inequality. As a race, it appears that are we going round and round on the same merry-go-round learning nothing from history, merely changing the players and their titles.

Today, has wealth and power been concentrated into the hands of the few, just as in the feudal lords of the City States of Europe? Have the CEO's of our transnational businesses substituted the Barons of Medieval times? Have we learnt nothing better? Are we destined to continue to replay the same dramas? Has anything changed at the collective unconscious or conscious level? Is there evidence of ethical or emotional change that is progressive?

I will now explore some of the challenges that can arise when human principles are absent.

The Negative Model

The absence of humane principles in the culture of an organisation ensures not only the lack of influence by them but leads to an unhealthy environment, rife with all the things that can cause corruption and perversion. Additionally, at an individual level it causes conflict between those whose personal ethics operate at a higher standard than those who don't. The negative outcomes of the Principles' absence are much easier to see than the Principles' presence in an organisation. We can recognise symptoms and outcomes much easier than their root causes. It is important to trace such negative outcomes back to their source and make corrections there, rather than try and correct the thousands of problems that appear.

Whilst researching the world of work, one of the primary things that became clear is that if the principle of integrity is either non-operative or broken, deception and perversion come into play and become embedded in the culture in a variety of ways. If not strongly resisted, various levels of corruption become the norm in the system of an organisation. This has been exemplified by the Libor rigging and foreign exchange price fixings scandals that have been discovered in the financial markets. The presence of self-deception in many individuals allows corruption and then greed to have sway. Truth is not spoken, rules are not respected and the principles of justice and fairness are damaged. Distrust of the whole system then occurs internally and when discovered by others externally; widespread distrust of the organisation can lead to reputational damage and customer boycotts, leading to severe damage to its financial viability.

Figure 1. The negative outcomes of missing human principles

In considering the negative model above, reflect on how:

- A lack of truth leads to lies, self-deception, deceiving others and illusion of all kinds.
- A lack of respect leads to abuse, disrespect of others, and disrespect of systems, policies and procedures.

- No justice leads to unfair contracts, greed, unjust outcomes and abuse of the weak, or the unrepresented.
- A lack of respect and fairness at senior levels in organisations can generate insensitivity, hardheartedness and inhumane responses to personal needs.
- Lack of integrity at a personal level creates dishonesty, self-deception, deception of others, corruption and political manoeuvring.
- A lack of integrity at a company level leads to corruption, criminal activity, inconsistent standards, inconsistent behaviours, silos and conflicts.
- A lack of integrity at the top of an organisation can very quickly lead to corruption of various kinds in the whole system.
- An absence of trust leads to distrust, suspicion, reputational damage, negative customer reactions, isolation and separation.

Each principle not maintained by individuals or groups in an organisation has a resulting impact into the wider social and business environment... normally designated as the company culture.

- A breakdown of truth/honesty leads to the dissemination of lies as the norm.
- A lack of respect leads to abuse, lack of diversity and prejudice, most often evidenced by the exclusion of females or disabled persons in significant positions.
- A lack of justice and fairness allows greed to have reign with widening differentials as to

salaries, benefits and workplace distinctions that point to personal advantage driving decisions.

- A breakdown of trust leads to distrust, conflict and politicking for one's agenda.
- A lack of integrity allows deception and corruption to thrive in small or large, depending on context and circumstance.
- Not taking responsibility for personal power, to act in a moral way, leads to abuse of power.
- Too much power in too few hands leads to far-reaching corruption.

In what country that had to bail out its banks, do its people not feel that they have unfairly been penalised by a small group of people who acted deceptively and without integrity to benefit themselves?

Where there is little integrity, there is a failure of character and in our work environments there will be a lack of respect in the whole infrastructure of inter-personal dealings. This will generate a culture that grows unhealthy environments where respect, truth, trust and justice will be missing.

In order to reverse the negative cycle, certain specific questions need to be asked. If organisations were to try and start brand new, to build a new culture — a substance in which things could grow — what will they have in it and what will they not have? What standards would they wish to see in the world? What injustice or unfairness would they wish to correct?

Many people have NOT received an education on the meaning of Truth, Respect, Justice, Trust, Integrity and Power. They have used these terms and have perhaps a skimpy understanding of what each of these words may mean. If they could understand their relevance and recognise that they need to be strongly integrated into the business realms, they would promote their importance. They would see the need to understand their full meaning, as well as the integration of them into the fabric of business processes.

The Humanity Principles Model

There have been many voices exhorting the need for agreed standards of behaviours for business. There are calls for lawyers to take up the mantle to ensure full adherence to the law, but the foundations of good character are missing in many places. It is as if a building is being built upon shifting sands, rather than steel posts well inserted deep into the bedrock. The Humanity Principles are the equivalent of the steel posts of good human character. In their absence, poor attitudes and character weaknesses prevail; people are considered disposable and are treated as such.

On the basis that we can grow, learn and improve and that we are evolving a better consciousness with each century, with understandings and behaviours that value human beings, a new model is presented through which modern business can be examined.

> *"You can never change things by fighting the existing reality. To change something, build a new model that makes the existing model obsolete."*

Buckminster Fuller

This model suggests a new business *modus operandi...*

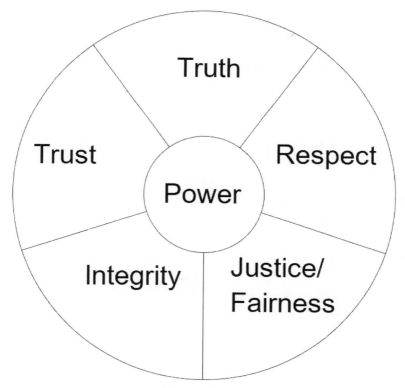

Figure 2. The Humanity Principles

There are five fundamental principles that if adhered to and lived, will anchor a person into an ethical and moral life; Truth, Respect, Justice, Trust and Integrity. It is easier to adopt these into our personal lives as these principles have subconsciously been ingrained into most people. The sixth principle,

Power is part of the life force and active content in all people, which needs to be liberated in order for the other five to operate successfully. The Humanity Principles Model has Power at its centre, because without Power, a person cannot act on behalf of, or implement the Principles. It is personal power and personal responsibility that comes from power that enables a person to act on anything at all!

A business however, does not have these ingrained principles, nor does it have the capacity to function by them, in the same way that it doesn't have the capacity to think for itself. What it has instead are the rules and regulations that provide the boundaries of its operation and corporate governance structures that dictate its formation and going on. It is human beings who work in companies that can adopt such principles and dictate where and how they are to be expressed. It is for them that the book is written and to whom the following is addressed.

There are many cross-supporting ideas that bind the six principles together and even though here the focus is on one Principle at a time, the fibres of our humanity interlink and fuse these principles together, making an impact on each other, not just sequentially, but across the model.

I will describe each of the Principles and then give some examples of how they can be applied.

- If a person knows the truth, hears the truth and speaks the truth, they can be said to be honest and therefore can easily be transparent in their interactions with others. They will have self-respect and build self-trust. They will engage in behaviours that that will lead others to respect and trust them.

- If a person has self-respect and they respect others, they will tell the truth to them and will want to hear the truth in return, because they appreciate that honesty and openness belongs with being respectful. By aligning with truth and respect, fairness and justice follows. If they respect themselves then they will naturally respect others.

- If a person wants justice to prevail, they will seek to be just and fair in all transactions, interactions and relationships and for equality for both parties, with regards to responsibilities and rewards. Fairness creates balance internally and externally (which is why the scales are traditionally used as the symbol for justice).

- If a person wants to be trusted, they need to have demonstrated an adhesion to truth, respect and fairness in their behaviours consistently over a length of time, so that others can form accurate expectations of response. What people or organisations can specifically be trusted for mostly relates to previous consistently demonstrated examples of behaviour and results.

- If a person has integrity, it is because they have a set of ethics and principles that they are conscious of and will have adhered to in a consistent manner over an extended period of time. This relates to being truthful, respectful, fair and just so they trust themselves, and so are clear that they have Integrity. Integrity means acting in accordance with the principles that they have put in place in themselves.

- All humans have power by reason of their existence – power comes through the life force that gives them life. In life and work we exercise that power through self-responsibility and accountability. Power enables exertion – the energy to do and accomplish whatever it is in our choice, possibility or mandate to do. Power provides the choice to practise and live by humane principles or not. And, occasionally, we must use power to stop perversion and abuse of these principles taking place and to insist on their activation into the culture or process that may be operating without them.

- In the context of work, the exercise of personal power ensures that justice and fairness appear in the agreements and contracts that we or our organisation they are responsible for, that clearly describe both parties' responsibilities and recompense.

Each of us adheres to the humanity principles by virtue of our thoughts, attitudes, mindset, our values and therefore our behaviour. If there is coherence between them all we feel comfortable in ourselves that we are in integrity. All of this together creates a powerful influence on what we will do and what we won't do.

How to Use The Principles

The Principles should sit alongside the business basics of creating products, services, marketing them, administration, management and HR matters – all the business processes that are currently practiced. They should be used as a reference point, to assess "How" the business processes are being done. For example, if a decision is to be taken on where a product will be produced, when considering the options, the Humanity Principles can be called on as a reference for evaluating the options available. 'Does the potential manufacturer practice respect for their employees? What are the normal working hours for the factory and for each employee? What is the quality of the working environment? Is it clean, supportive and humane? Are children less than 16 or 18 employed? Are fair wages being paid? Does the rate for production of the product allow for fair wages to be paid? Are you, the organisation too demanding in the rates you are willing to pay? What is the truth of what you are being told and what you could actually find out?

If such principles are adopted into the fabric and ongoing processes of an organisation, then they will benefit not only the human beings using them, but also the people about whom they are deciding. They will improve the working lives of many more people. The evidence for this is manifold from those few organisations already practising in part these principles.

The aim for the model is to help people take decisions on a principled and therefore ethical basis. It can be used in an active way to identify the dilemmas that confront a decision making process, by considering whether Truth, Respect, Justice/Fairness, Integrity and Trust may be being ignored or contravened. Using the model facilitates an awareness of people and their participation in the various stages of business processes.

It projects companies into adopting a more socially democratic system involving more people; it will lead to improved performances all around; as key players are included in, their loyalty and commitment to the activity will increase, as will their productivity.

The Model calls for new learning and development of an organisation's leaders. These principles must not be theoretical ideas that have no practise attached to them. Leaders rising to the top of FTSE companies may find it hard to recognise a need to learn new models, new ways of thinking and new ways of doing. Some FTSE 100 companies still deny the value or need for a Corporate Social responsibility agenda or a Code of Conduct, and the Humanity Principles may represent a challenge to the current thinking and operating of their business. This model is part of a new movement taking place in our world today – to create a more equal and fair society and economy – by creating a sustainable shared prosperity.

The Model calls for Enlightened leaders, those visionary individuals who can see the value that such principles can bring to our world; who are prepared to step up to meet the standards the Principles call for. Engagement, commitment and loyalty are the natural resultants and outcomes of applying the Humanity Principles. Enlightened leaders can recognise that implementing such Principles into their sphere of influence will mean improving the conduct and standards of the people in their organisation. By implementing the Principles, they will create standards that impact their organisation's contracts with suppliers, with customers and their local community. It will move their organisation's influence outside the boundaries of itself, to engage with parties who have the power to make their organisation even more successful.

If leaders continue to aim at success through competition, on the competitive roulette wheel of difference, challenge and the divisive positioning where everyone is only looking out for themselves, breakdowns of trust, integrity and reputational damage can only be the resulting outcomes. The 'competitive mindset' closes down collaborative working opportunities of having many people, their experience and circumstances aligned to meeting your needs and your opportunities.

Each experience, problem or challenge that a person encounters that they filter through the principles can be refined to better reflect the learning and development of the person. As people, we do not come out fully formed, so these principles are constantly evolving whilst a person lives and works. Each Principle as its practised (eg., tell the truth, listen to the truth, hear the truth) goes to form the internal psyche of a person and as it's implemented in their activities, it grows their awareness and consciousness. The character of each person accumulates value as they live and they express themselves in the world. The range, extent and application of these humane principles can be growing amongst us as a race, as we collectively evolve our consciousness to better awareness and behaviour.

The Two Flows of The Humanity Model

The Humanity Principles model works in two flows. It flows positively from Truth, leading to Respect, leading to Justice/Fairness, leading to Integrity, leading to Trust where a person lives each quality and acts from those qualities. Power is at the heart of the positive cycle. Where power is distributed and taken up appropriately by all members of staff, human principles are enabled and can infuse relationships, contracts, processes and systems.

As more clearly explained before, when the Principles are ignored or break down, the flow goes backward, so where Truth is not spoken, Trust will be impacted and Distrust and suspicion will become rife. Where integrity fails, corruption can thrive and there will be no Trust. Without Integrity, Justice and Fairness may be ignored, and exploitation and abuse occur; where Justice or Fairness is absent, Respect will be non-operative, abuse will be allowed and lies, rather than truth will be spoken. This negative spiral damages respect and trust in all relationships and an unhealthy, toxic environment will result. At the centre of the negative model is No Accountability which a system without human principles will facilitate. The lack of personal accountability enables the negative outcomes to dictate the environment and allows behaviours to fall to the lowest common denominator.

Leaders within organisations can opt to enforce more personal responsibility and accountability of people's actions, ensuring that individuals can face the negative consequences of their actions and more quickly adopt human principles to build the positive cycle. Bad behaviour must be identified, highlighted and penalised. Good behaviours that build the positive cycle need to be recognised and rewarded.

What follows are the detailed observations regarding each of the Principles and how to practically use them to institute them as ways of thinking and doing within a business context. Multiple examples are offered of people who have demonstrated various aspects of each principle and how that has played out in their environment.

Chapter Five

TRUTH

Truth to mean: A statement that expresses what is, or has been, in an unbiased, neutral and uncoloured way. It conveys clean information that adds to the body of knowledge and awareness of people.

Honesty to mean: imparting truthful statements by a person without any designs of deceiving, misdirecting, manipulating or misinforming others.

The desire for Truth is an innate programme in human beings. If we think of the human body and how it operates, so much of it is automated – it needs to sleep, eat, process food and extract energy, it thinks, moves, and breathes – all of these functions operate successfully by themselves. We get to intercept our needs and desires to some degree with some of them, for example by choosing what we eat or what we choose to expend the energy on, but for the most part, automated activities happen in us and for us.

The need for Truth is as much automated in us, as the need to breathe. The need to know what is true or false is embedded in our DNA, along with the need to grow. As we grow up the innate programme to learn, to know, to understand what things are and how they work expedites us to greater and greater learning. As specie, the need to know the Truth has helped us evolve out of being hunters for food for survival, to create societies, housing, education, philosophy, art, culture, technology, theatre and all aspects of growth and evolution.

It is as if Truth is nourishment to us, enabling us to understand and connect to what is real and viable, whereas lies are toxic to our minds and systems, in the same way that lies in relationships are toxic to the people in that relationship. A common saying is 'The truth will set you free' and in my experience and many others who I have coached, the dissemination of lies in a workplace builds up a toxicity that doesn't allow them to know what is true. People would prefer to hear the truth, however horrible, uncomfortable or unfortunate it is going to be in its ramifications. They much prefer it to the confusion and darkness that lies perpetuate.

Executives appreciate working with me outside of their work context, often because it is easier to speak truthfully of their situation, and our conversations often resonate in a clear way that enables them to connect to what is true.

A group of executives generating lies and deception – for example as happened at Enron — leads to all kinds of toxicity both within the organisation (in its employees and their relationships) and outside (for its suppliers, shareholders, customers). Lies lead to all kinds of economic costs, not just to the people employed by the organisation but to the organisation itself. The fraudulent activity at Enron was perpetuated from the systems within the organisation, to its energy suppliers, energy customers and the stock market in which it was listed, creating huge economic burdens that other people were forced to pay. Lies and fraud go together – building a partnership that brings benefits to the defrauder — whilst inflicting costs upon those being defrauded.

When Truth is valued and practised within businesses — clarity in relationships, honesty in contracts and arrangements with surety of outcomes are the result. When executives don't speak the Truth or invite truthful feedback from others, half-truths, lies and ultimately fraud will be the result, and may escalate to economic and emotional cost.

Not all organisations emphasise a requirement for truth in their dealings and operations. Businesses mostly leave issues of truth to the personal determination of its officers and people, assuming that honesty is a standard characteristic of people. It is rare for businesses to require staff to behave with truth and honesty as a standard. They may infer it, but rarely plainly state that they require it. It is encouraging to encounter the John Lewis Partnership Rules which are sprinkled throughout with advocacy for Truth, Respect and Fairness. As an example: Rule 49. "Partners must be scrupulously honest in their dealings with the Partnership and with each other, and never seek to gain from the Partnership any more than they sincerely believe is fair." Such a rule requires behaviours that reflect not just honesty, but scrupulous honesty – honesty flavoured with justice and fairness.

When communications are made with a focus on communicating what is true, rather than with a spin to manipulate people, it leads to honest responses that enable leaders to gain an accurate view of the situation. More accurate information determines better decisions. More honesty in any situation facilitates more Truth to appear, allowing participants to communicate openly, inputting relevant information and adding to the whole matter under consideration. By people sharing what is personally true and honest for them, it enables the best collective Truth to become clear. It is through the sharing of views that a collective intelligence on what is the best response can naturally appear. Enlightened leaders are able to ask for the truth, listen to the truth and hear the truth, however personally distressing it is, because they know that the outcome of such a process will generate better information and decisions than they could have come to on their own.

As people, we value Truth and mostly respect people who tell us the truth, because they demonstrate respect for us when they tell us the truth. We prefer to deal with truth as a currency of exchange. Truth abhors dishonesty and hypocrisy. A person who holds to what is true and speaks the Truth, will much more likely be honest. The John Lewis Partnership in their 2014 Annual Report recognised that there is a move to "radical transparency", meaning customers, Non-Governmental Organisations ('NGOs') and the Media have access to more information about what company organisations do and customers can easily post comments and be influenced by other customers' views when making purchasing decisions. They recognised how important it was to provide the truth on a whole range of subject matter that keeps customers informed about their thinking, approach and demonstrated values. Customers want to know 'who' they are buying from, just as much as 'what' they are buying.

The Human Body and Truth

The human mind is programmed to process truth. When truth is spoken and heard, a person's mind is able to process the ideas and concepts that are presented with ease and there is no interruption or hiccup in their system. When a person hears lies, somewhere in their system, they know that it is not correct and a dissonance is felt. An analogy to describe processing truth is like us drinking water which our body is well capable of processing easily, passing through our body, providing hydration, then passing out safely.

Lies are like putting lubricating oil of a car into the human system. They are as damaging to a person as drinking that lubricating oil. Lies are an introduction of toxins to our mental and emotional systems which they are not designed to process, and which, if we take on too much, damages us. It's natural for a person's mind and body to baulk at a lie or untruth. When a person knows (perhaps subconsciously) that they are being asked to accept a lie for truth, they often experience an acute sensitivity that something is not quite right, even though they may not be able to put their finger on what specifically is false.

In cases where a person is suffering from self-deception, they may be unconscious of the fact that they are lying, but others hearing them will often recognise untruths, however much the person may believe what they are saying.

What I have come to see is that when a person consistently lies and does not speak the truth, they will experience fear in themselves. At first fear is a fleeting awareness of anxiety, but then it becomes a background constant state that colours much of their experience. Fear is there because they recognise in the depths of their real selves that they are lying to themselves and to others and they fear being found out. Something in them recognises the hypocrisy of representing themselves as one thing, knowing that underneath they believe in something else entirely. Undoubtedly there comes a time when the truth will out and all the lies and self-deceptions they've been being, and giving out, come back to haunt them and they have to confront their dishonesty.

This may not be true for corporate psychopaths however, as identified by Professor Clive Boddy, author of *Corporate Psychopaths: Organisational Destroyers*. He identifies some of the main characteristics of corporate psychopaths as liars with a lack of empathy, single minded ambition and lack of remorse for their actions. Driven to gain prestige, money and power, they will use their charm to manipulate those above them to gain promotion and demonstrate their psychopathic tendencies to everyone below them, using lies, abuse and bullying to cause chaos, toxicity and destruction of relationships and wellbeing. Organisations beware— perpetuating lies are the main characteristic of such people!

When considering Truth, a responsible person will ask the question "Is this true because it is a fact, circumstance or reality now, today, this moment?" Or, is it a story that a person has been told or told themselves, or a story that has been perpetuated by other people before them?

One such story that I have heard repeated many times during the process of writing this book is that "a business' primary objective is to make money" and secondarily "to deliver value/dividends to shareholders". Yet these are statements that hide the truth, which is that businesses exist for many reasons, and should contribute to the betterment of our world, including the betterment of its staff, its customers, its suppliers and the planet (at minimum by not damaging its environment). Another truth that such statements hide is that some organisations are run to benefit their most senior executives, whether by huge salaries and benefits, or, by allowing them free rein to exercise their power hungry personalities and in a few cases, their psychopathic tendencies.

As Maslow* has outlined, there is a hierarchy of needs that people fulfil through work. Once physiological and safety needs are met, people look to satisfy the need to belong, create self-esteem and self-actualise. Work is an important arena within which such needs can be met. In the developed world, people want to have a better reason for why they work than to generate profits for shareholders. They need a higher purpose for working than just to make money. People whose basic survival needs have been met need an environment which enables them to work doing what brings out their talents and fully engages their capabilities. They need to know that their work contributes to making the world a better place, for themselves and for other people. People living well above the poverty line need better, more meaningful reasons for working.

Truth and The Media

In today's business world, in what manner of life or work is truth valued as a principle of operation? Where so much information is massaged for mass consumption and manipulated to represent the best "spin" that can be placed upon it? I have been in many conversations with responsible business people who say "there is no truth any more, there are only peoples' opinions and what we say about our business is the truth, because that is our opinion".

In the context of the media, the truth is sometimes very hard to find or determine. The media, whether PR, advertising, or even journalism, has often been an agency for perpetuating non-truths or various views that the company might like to be true but often are not. Whole industries work to create advertisements, jingles, marketing strategies, images and myths that promote ideas that they want other people (you and me) to have. Some of these ideas focus on making you feel good – Coca Cola, McDonalds etc. – as they attempt to manipulate your emotional states causing you to want to buy products in order to gain that 'feeling good' emotion again and again. Sometimes, advertisements promote a way of seeing a product they are trying to sell as totally opposite to what is true. Pay day loan company' adverts promote the idea of convenience to access money but fail to point out the possible exorbitant costs associated with a loan that may result in extraordinary inconveniences!

In the world of work, truth as an important principle or quality is rarely sought – rather, organisations prefer to create figments of information about themselves and their place in the world — without considering how much they are half-truths or even outright lies. These appear on our TV screens and newspapers as adverts or promotions, creating images and stories that present companies' products and services in the best way. We experience them as branding, advertisements, sales and marketing strategies, promotions, internet websites, webinars and TV adverts.

It seems that the pursuit of truth in the arena of business has either been assumed, or given up as its value has been forgotten or lost. People have become so used to being manipulated and manipulating others that it has become acceptable. One would think that journalists and news programmes would be interested to track down the truth and represent it in their newspapers and TV programmes, but 'drama' and heightened 'angles to stories' now often distort the truth in order to promote a 'hue and cry' about some matter that then hides what may be true. It panders to a simplistic manipulation of people's emotions in order that they then react and speak about it, and want to buy more papers, or see their programme again. This 'drama creation' is featured as a marketing strategy by companies who want potential customers to raise 'a drama' about them. All of this noise, this buzz, hides the truth.

Where can we look for truth and why should we? What place does truth play in our lives? The things that just are, for example in nature — the sun shines, it rains, day becomes night, night becomes day — these are things that happen that we take for granted. We do not feel we have to attribute a meaning to them happening. These facts/truths are neutral and for most people this level of truth can be agreed upon without dispute. Natural truth doesn't carry the filters of personal emotion, advertisement, hype or spin. Whereas the mass of products and services that have been created to sell to people, were created from the requirement to make money and these are injected with a mass of emotion to persuade and influence people to buy.

All of these media utilities are used to promote an image of what the organisation would like you to believe was true about itself. Whether they actually are a true representation of it depends upon whether the organisation values Truth and Integrity and practises them in its representations to the world; or whether it is practicing manipulation in order to sell its products or services to the world without any consideration of deeper principles.

The truth is important in our world so we can see a deeper reality than the face value representations that people make to us about them, their products or services.

If a human is designed to process and recognise the truth, corporations are not created with this standard at all. Many efforts of business to manufacture information about itself, its products and activities, may actually be perpetuating and feeding lies to its employees and its customers. How can they tell which is which? Such representations may be outright lies that a business is willing to make, that quite literally may be poisonous to its consumers (tobacco corporations come to mind here). Many corporations operating within an inhumane feeling environment are willing to pay the price of causing illness and damage to their consumers and see that as part of the price of doing business.

It's like a packet of cigarettes – inside are sticks of poison that on the outside the Surgeon General warns may be poisonous and damaging to a person's health, yet millions of people see the warning, open the pack and smoke the cigarettes. There is no warning about the power to damage that corporations can have upon the health and well-being of employees, consumers, customers or suppliers. It is quite possible that they can do as much damage – thalidomide, Rena Plaza, Bhopal, Three Mile Island and many other instances of organisations harming hundreds of thousands and even millions of people by their products and processes and not acknowledging or accepting the truth of their culpability and making restitution.

Employees at work are confronted by the requirement to represent things as better than they are. They are made to feel that they cannot tell the truth because the truth is not good enough, not as good as it could be or should be, in line with the organisations previous marketing representations.

So Why Is Truth Important at Work?

- Truth is important if an organisation wants to be fair in its dealings with its employees, its customers, its suppliers, and its interactions with the world. Fairness can only be correctly assessed if the truth of a situation is known. Untruth biases the case to one side or another.

- Truth is important if an organisation wants to meet its contracts and obligations in a just way. If misrepresentations of what is true are made by one side or another then a just or fair contract cannot be come to, as one side is weighting their side of the negotiation.

- Truth is important if an organisation doesn't want to be a hypocrite in the world ie.,to represent itself in one way and yet to behave in ways that are contrary to what it asserts to be true. Even organisations with 'values' can do this; they say they value their customers, whilst exploiting them. Reflecting on what the Truth is avoids behaving this way.

- Truth is important when it is allowed to act as a mirror to reflect the real/deeper motivations, meanings and reasons why some things are done and why others are not done. Including acknowledging the truth of greed as a motivator of actions taken or not taken.

- Truth is important as the touchstone of reality when spin, advertisement and hype have made everyone lost inside the fictions that have been created by an organisation and its media machine.

- Truth is important if a business wants itself and its employees to act with integrity in how they say people should behave, including its leaders, managers and staff and have established ways for holding them to account.

An Example

One evening, whilst writing this book, I watched *'The Most Dangerous Man in America'* a documentary on the release of the Pentagon Papers by Daniel Ellensberg. It is a fascinating story of a man who acted within the American political infrastructure to prosecute the Vietnamese war, whilst knowing very early on that actions were being taken on the basis of lies. Daniel Ellensburg worked for the U.S. government, under Lyndon Johnson, and in his role, he fabricated evidence to suggest that Vietnam was attacking and hurting U.S. soldiers, thus expediting the Vietnam War. He knew these lies were compounded by more lies and even more lies. The creation of these lies did not seem to cause him concern at this stage of his career. (The prosecution of atrocities and violence upon the Vietnamese people went on in total for 25 years.)

The documentary outlines the journey he made from accepting the lies he helped promulgate, to meeting people who were prepared to go to prison for the sake of truth and peace; to confronting his own internal lies, which had enabled him to live with the self-deception of supporting those who were lying to the American people as a whole. By acknowledging the truth and being willing to pay the price of making the truth public, (he released large amounts of Pentagon Papers to the media for which he was prosecuted), he enabled the truth to be published by at least 17 newspapers, despite the U.S. government seeking injunctions against those newspapers.

By confronting the truth of what he did and in remorse for his lies, he made available the Pentagon papers to the newspapers, and in atonement, accepted the punishment of being put on trial and going to jail.

The film's focus on truth and lies highlighted that a penalty needs to be paid if lies are knowingly perpetuated. Sometimes speaking the truth also exacts a penalty – of uncomfortability of being at difference with others and of standing out. It confronts each of us with the price that we will pay to make the truth known to ourselves and to act in accordance with that truth.

One of the legal experts that spoke about the ramifications of the legal case enabling the New York Times and Washington Post newspapers to publish the then-classified Pentagon Papers without risk of government censorship or punishment, was that it created legal precedents for the First Amendment on the rights of the individual for freedom to speak out against their government. Justice Hugo Black opinion elaborated on the absolute superiority of the First Amendment, confirming that:

"In the First Amendment the Founding Fathers gave the free press the protection it must have to fulfil its essential role in our democracy. The press was to serve the governed, not the governors. The Government's power to censor the press was abolished so that the press would remain forever free to censure the Government. The press was protected so that it could

*bare the secrets of government and inform the people.
Only a free and unrestrained press can effectively
expose deception in government. Paramount among the
responsibilities of a free press is the duty to prevent any
part of the government from deceiving the people and
sending them off to distant lands to die of foreign
fevers and foreign shot and shell."*

Most FTSE listed companies in the UK and Fortune
500 Companies in the US have what are called
'Whistleblower lines' which are telephone lines manned
by external companies to take information from
employees that may disclose bad behaviour, fraud and
corruption that may be taking place within their
companies. This is excellent, and is a part of a process
to allow for truth to be revealed, but protecting
whistleblowers once they have come forward is not yet
a safe and secure process. Whistleblowers are likely to
face discrimination, prejudice and attack from others
around them and to have the force of the whole
company against them.

The right of individuals to speak the truth and to
disclose the lies that big corporations or governments
could perpetrate upon the people of the world must be
valued and protected. They should be appreciated and
promoted, both within the personal domain of
individuals and within the public domains of corporate
activity and public office.

Truth and Leadership

How many leaders encourage an environment where
the truth can be spoken and heard, without
defensiveness or attack resulting upon the person who

speaks it? How many leaders positively discourage the speaking of truth, and perpetuate a culture of grey innuendos and political "yes" people supporting one version of what is promoted as the truth? What is the truth of this matter in your organisation? What processes are active in your organisation to enable employees to speak the truth to your managers and leaders?

In conversations with executives, I observed that truth was often assumed and rarely challenged or actively sought. Other people's opinions were discounted if volunteered and not sought if they weren't, as there wasn't openness to the idea that Truth might come from people below their level. Information gathering systems that allowed for the passing on of information upwards were often ramshackle and inadequate. Leaders are mostly concerned with the downward flow of information – what they want their employees to understand — rather than what their employees can tell them. Truth speaking is not welcomed, valued or protected when it happens, as it often points out what leaders and senior staff are doing that they should not be doing.

What truths needed to be spoken, that were spoken, which caused apartheid to fail in South Africa? Powerful things happen when a mass of people give up holding onto one view of a truth eg., "apartheid is a fair and appropriate way for a country to organise its people, who are different because of colour and race and that it is best to keep them separate" and take on a different truth that says "all human beings (whatever their colour or race) are equal and must have the same rights as all other human beings, whatever their colour, race or religious alignment." Taking on a new truth, is an act of enlightenment that comes from letting in more truth into the situation. It enables more people to give up their attachment to their personal view in order to take on a higher truth.

Pragmatically, when people are in conflict on what the truth is, they should revert to the principle of Respect in order to listen carefully to each other's truth and to see if they can both change their perception to see a different or new truth. If the truth is not clear, a person can move into honesty and say, 'well this is my truth, but I am open to the idea that honestly you may have a different view and I am open to see a different truth'. What is important and valuable about this principle is the love of the idea of truth; the openness to see beyond one's personal opinion, the wish to see beyond one's personal perspective, to perceive a greater truth that can provide greater nourishment.

ENLIGHTENED LEADERS PERSPECTIVE

Truth that is connected to a deeper generic truth about our existence here on this planet and how we should deal with each other, offers nourishment and well-being. The desire for truth should operate as a stronger imperative above the desire to be right, because the more truth we connect to, the greater well-being we have.

Higher truths resonate in more people – so that more people can relate to that truth and recognise its validity. Opinions tend to resonate to groups who have previous cultural exposure to that opinion. Truth carries greater accuracy and description of what is real. The more truths that can be encompassed about a situation, the better the decision making can occur. Enlightened leaders seek for greater truths, therefore they will consult with more people, hear more sides to an issue, ponder more to gain deeper insights into the factors surrounding that issue and the consequences of their decisions.

To aid in this process, Truth Seeking Questions at the end of this chapter are designed to help.

The following questions prompt self-seeking truths in individuals or groups. When you feel uncomfortable or resistant to either considering the question or applying it to the issue you are currently thinking about, it is a sign that you are either avoiding the truth, or are practising self-deception. This tells you that it is by focusing on those specific questions that you will uncover truths that will help you the most.

By presenting some of these questions in relation to an issue or concern to a group or team in a forum discussion, you will be surprised at the range of perceptions, insights and awareness that others can bring to the matter. It is an extraordinary experience for most leaders firstly to allow themselves to (in their terms) be vulnerable and ask others for their opinion, and secondly to experience the broad-ranging differences of awareness that can derive from different people!

TRUTH SEEKING QUESTIONS:

1. What evidence is there that what I think about this issue/matter problem is true?
2. What do you / others think?
3. What am I not taking into account that would lead me to a different truth?
4. What are we not considering that would suggest a different truth?
5. How open am I to see bigger truths than what I currently perceive?
6. If I can make better decisions, does it matter who provides the ideas and insights that are different to mine?
7. How can I know that what I think /you say is true?
8. How can I know that what I think/you say is false?
9. Whose views do I discount and invalidate because I don't like them?
10. Am I making the truth or my ego more important?

Chapter Six

RESPECT

Respect to mean: To view a person or thing in order to find value, to give recognition and to deal with them equitably. To look again, not to be familiar with, not to dismiss or take for granted. To value and esteem the person, their contribution and their presence.

Respect for The Individual

The holding and giving of respect to other human beings is the starting point for good standards and behaviours. We are all born equal, whatever our race, creed, gender, ability or disability. Respect is a quality that one both extends to others and receives from others.

In the workplace, Respect for people's humanity is vital for ensuring that employees are given the best chance to succeed and to use their best abilities. Respect creates esteem. Self-respect creates self-esteem.

When respect is combined with truth, relationships thrive with truthful and honest conversations, open and supportive dealings. When people adhere to the truth and extend respect it allows them to challenge each others' views, knowing that it is safe and they won't have to deal with adverse negative reactions, nor that the relationship will be damaged as a result. Respect with challenge fosters open dealings without fear.

To company leaders I would ask — do your employees feel good about your company? Are they proud of working for it? Does it raise their self-esteem because they do? Is their self-esteem raised by the way that their leaders and managers manage and lead them? They are very likely to be positive in all their answers if they are respected for who they are and the talents they contribute are recognised and used.

If however, an organisation experiences conflicts and differences in its people because its senior managers or departments are at war, then this is a clue that respect is not being extended to people. Why does respect seem such a hard quality to build into the working patterns, behaviours and systems of some organisations? Yet in others I have experienced, respect is easily extended, sustained and maintained by living consistently the policies and values that its leaders have set down. If respect for people is a standard and required behaviour in a business environment, it almost always means a respect and compliance for policies and systems in that organisation also.

A culture of respect or disrespect is mostly generated by managers or leaders by the quality of their interactions with each other and with those with whom they work. If senior managers actively disrespect each other, their hostilities create dysfunctional relationships and processes that make work very hard for those employees around them, or they create cultures of fear and blame, making employees feel unsafe. Such disrespectful behaviours lead to atmospheric toxicity and cross-fires that seriously damage others around them.

Case Study

Where respect is advocated but not lived, the following case study demonstrates what can happen:

Two leaders disrespected each other, criticised and judged each other, created differences and difficulties for people around them, and most especially those who reported to them. This regularly resulted in problems ending up with the Head of HR. The active disrespect between the two executives generated conflicts amongst their teams which were difficult to sort out because of the entrenched positions of their respective bosses. He found it extremely hard to mediate as neither party was willing to compromise or change their mindset. After a year of putting up with this, and failing to resolve the differences, he resigned. What he could have done but didn't, in order to save some shred of dignity for himself, was to take the organisation to court for extreme stress and aggravation. The avowed values of the organisation even recognised the importance of respect, yet the executive team never openly discussed the problem, never discussed this flagrant abuse of their values or challenged these two executives to change their behaviours.

I was asked to help. The first thing I did was have the Executive team undertake a psychometric assessment that highlighted each person's strengths. In joint session, I highlighted how each person's strengths complemented each others, how each person should be respected and appreciated for the unique contributions they could make. I then openly spoke about the conflict problems that two of them had and encouraged everyone to speak about it — their experience of it, the results it was causing in their team, in the organisation as a whole, — which helped to have the problem aired in communal session. It was not allowed to fester. The two executives in conflict could no longer go around pretending that their differences weren't having negative impacts. They adjusted their behaviours. This helped!

Nelson Mandela as a child learnt an important lesson whilst being brought up in his Uncle's Court. He learnt the importance of respect; both that he was worthy of respect, and deserved to be treated with respect, and that he should respect other human beings. Everyone who ever met him, commented on his respectful and humane manner, making each person he dealt with feel wonderful. It was this very important awareness that led to his non-violent approach that endured for most of his leadership in the ANC prior to his imprisonment. It was only at the last when this non-violence failed to gain progress that he gave in and allowed activities that brought harm to people, and not just to property.

When I discuss the issue of respect with executives they explain that they struggle between being very task-focused, driven and controlling (a way that many of them say they have to be, 'to get things done') and being humane (taking time to be interested in people and their lives and 'having social conversations'). Many say they find it difficult to do both — and often because of their own preference, they will predominate on one side or the other. The consideration of Respect as an issue doesn't come into their awareness, on either side of the task-focus or the people-focus spectrum. They translate respect as being seen to be caring and interested, rather than genuinely being respectful of people's lives and what they might need to live and work constructively.

Respect sits in the middle between task focus and people focus, and has to apply to both. It calls for a middle way of caring about people as individuals who have a life outside of work, with talents and skills that they wish to apply in the service of work; who are there working for you as equals, equally as interested to do what needs doing, rather than needing to be patronised or manipulated in order to do good work.

This is why work-life balance comes into the field of respect, because human beings have lives that need nourishing and supporting. Work that calls for individuals to work 10 to 12 hours a day or more, saps the well-being and sustenance of their lives, requiring them to draw energy and attention away from their family, friends, fun and play – all of the things that nurture well-being and balance – and apply them to work. This is gross unfairness.

Companies demonstrate respect for people and their contribution when they expect people to work for the number of hours they pay them, and not more. Many organisations have employment contracts with people that are patently false; where a person's contracted salary is based upon them working a 37-hour week, but in actuality, they regularly work 50 or 60 or more hours each week. They are not paid overtime, nor are their hours offset by them being allowed to take time off in recompense. Such contracts could be considered abusive, but many professional services firms in particular, rely on such unwritten contracts to function and to deliver the high benefits paid to the partner owners.

Respect for people and their contribution is demonstrated when you share the profits and benefits equitably. Fair and just distribution of profits in particular for owner-owned businesses is rare, though there are wide and various levels practiced. It is notable that only one law firm has been in the Sunday Times Top 100 Companies to Work For consistently over the last twelve years, namely Mills & Reeve LLP and it has a reputation for a strong valued led culture and a more equitable distribution of profits.

At the higher end of traditional corporate organisations, the issue becomes blurred by the high salaries that are paid to senior managers and directors, who are pressured because of this, to put the company and its requirements first; above the work-life balance of the individual, above the needs of their family, and often above their own health and wellbeing. In such cases, close to 70 hours per week or more are required of their lives to meet the requirements of the company's profitability.

Respect for Employees

If leaders were to spend some of their time in Board meetings considering what there is to respect in their people and thinking through all the humane issues relating to them and their employment in the company, rather than solely looking at numbers, economics and the bottom line, they might create even better results in business performance.

If executives considered every employee as a volunteer – who is contributing their life and precious time to engage in fulfilling the company's mission – then they would perceive their people very differently. They would certainly respect them more. For the truth is that each person could choose not to work for that organisation and work for another. Some managers' assumption that 'people only work here to gain a salary and do not have much choice' is disrespectful and demeaning.

If you respect a person, you don't infantilise them — you respect that they are an adult – and don't "protect them from the truth" or 'mollycoddle' them. Employees want to be seen as equal partners to executives and want to be told the truth of the company's situation at all times, so they can take up a fair share of the burden of growing their business. By sharing the burden, they quite fairly are interested to share the profits. By including them, executives allow for the opportunity of their employees helping them beyond their contracted engagement. Executives who don't want to keep their employees informed suggest that accurate information might impact morale, or they don't even consider it and don't disclose all that they could, because it is this that justifies their huge salaries. This is being disrespectful to employees.

Board members and senior executives consider their employees as workers operating at levels way below their concern and do not feel the need to include or communicate to them about the issues that they are struggling with. In fact, executives spend more time considering the delivery of information to City analysts than to their own employees.

This is in direct opposition to the stance adopted within the John Lewis Partnership, where Rule 50 says "Partners must respect and be courteous to each other and to anyone else with whom they have dealings on behalf of the Partnership. The Partnership will do all it can to encourage good personal relationships between Partners at all levels." Such a rule laid down and highlighted throughout the behaviours, styles and demonstrations of leaders and managers enforces Respect for employees and peers.

What level of respect to themselves and their lives do executives pay that could set the example to their employees? When I've coached some senior leaders in multi-national businesses, I have sometimes felt that they are way out of balance, in their willingness to give up their Sundays to travel to international meetings, to sacrifice their Friday nights and Saturdays, arriving back from international meetings; as well as all the nights and days away from their families. Having done this myself in my thirties, the excitement and ego importance that these travels generated made me feel vital and energised. I fly business class and occasionally in first class, and it certainly strokes your ego in a huge way! After eight years of this, I recognised how mad it was and what a great price I was paying in the diminishment of my family life. The respect I paid to my whole life as against just my business life and my own well-being was minimal; and to my family even less.

However, for many executives I speak with, the level of commitment of life and energy, inherent in 12 or 14 hour days, and weekend work is a fair recompense for the large salaries they are paid. The price of heart attacks, chronic fatigue and burnout is not calculated into their equation however.

When staff members are evaluated on their performance, it speaks volumes about the characteristics of the organisation for which they work. What we measure, we improve. What we ignore, we don't value. Having seen many competency frameworks of organisations, few aspects related to humanity make an appearance. Companies often have a Values piece on their competency frameworks – where managers assess whether their people behave in such ways:

'Praises, recognises and values individuals contributions and effort' or

'Treats people fairly without undue favouritism' or

'Demonstrates integrity, fairness and consistency, maintaining confidentiality and honesty in dealing with internal and external customers.'

Such behavioural statements are the concessions that organisations make to the values of humanity or ethical principles. There may be three or four statements on matters of humane dealings in 40 other statements relating to the hard aspects of performance.

Respect for Suppliers

Companies often have policies that are less than respectful to their suppliers eg., in terms and conditions and payment terms. Such disrespect is evident when employees use their positions of power to not return phone calls, respond to emails and generally make the supplier run around after them in order to win or sign up contracts. They make the supplier feel beholden to them, rather than it's an equal relationship that will lead to benefits for both of them.

When the quality of respect is lacking, the organisation's power is used to extract benefits for the organisation either by requesting discounts, or even monetary payments (such as the highly publicised case of Tesco). Suppliers are demeaned to the level of servants — there to serve as and when the client wants to use them.

Strong positive partnerships are where suppliers or vendors to the organisation are treated with respect, building long term opportunities for both parties. Both parties should recognise that they are creating opportunities that will lead to growing both businesses and both being profitable, with both parties sharing the risk and the profits. If suppliers cannot make a profit in working with you, then they don't have the money to invest in research and development to create more inspiring products for you and your business.

Respect for Diversity

In working with many companies, it became clear that some, by the very nature of what they did, had a predominance of men working for them. This certainly applied to construction companies, utility companies, merchants and traders, engineering, science and technology. In many of the older, well established firms, what went with these male-weighted companies was prejudice and bias against women, with general communication styles that unconsciously judged and denigrated them.

I spoke to women from these companies who reported that they were often spoken to in ways that were extremely inappropriate, being called 'girls' and generally spoken down to, treated as inferior, invalidated and dismissed. In some cases, these were Board members who were behaving like this!

I have encountered racial prejudice and behavioural conflicts that derive from differences in national characteristics and racial differences. I believe such differences, of gender, race and national characteristics to be filters of difference that are irrelevant, when considered from the humane perspective. However, where there is no respect, there is abuse; and lack of respect often leads to people believing that inequality is normal and acceptable. There are manifold instances of women being abused in business, with unequal pay, judgemental comments and chauvinistic behaviour. As well, there are many instances of racial prejudice and conflicts that arise from that. Enlightened leaders can change all this dramatically, by giving credence and respect to each person's humanity, and not focusing upon the differences.

Respect for The Organisation and its Purpose

The better the humanity principles are understood, promoted, advocated and adhered to by the executives within an organisation, the stronger the rationale becomes for an organisation to express its purpose more fully. Why does the organisation exist? What is the purpose and reason for its existence? What are its aims and principles? Who is to benefit by its existence and what value will it deliver to the world?

Purpose to mean: the fundamental reason why something exists, and the outcomes it seeks to create by its existence, through the actions it pursues and the manner in which it undertakes them.

Do executives think that they're in business to make money for themselves, to make money for the company and its shareholders, to provide a service or product to the world, or to make the world a better place? Are leaders respectful of the reason and purpose that their organisation exists and do they respect its existence? Certainly the leaders of Enron did not. The leaders and managers of the financial institutions that failed in the financial crisis did not. They did not respect the raison d'être of the organisation nor served to maintain its integrity. Whereas I see that some organisations do respect the reason why they were founded and seek continuously to maintain that. The stated purpose should truthfully address whom the organisation serves and the difference it seeks to make in the world.

I recently came across the following in a John Lewis store:

> *"When John Spedan Lewis created the John Lewis Partnership he set out our principles for doing business. His aim was to help bring a better quality of life to everyone in the company as well as to our customers. We stay true to that vision every day in these important, simple and rewarding ways:"*

and they go on to say what these ways are. The important point here is that they remain respectful of the originating purpose, whereas I'm aware that some charities for example, are coming under pressure from CEO's who have thrived amongst the cut and thrust of capitalism and are now employed by charities, who wish to make them 'commercial' and 'modern' ie., with less humane objectives.

Respect for The Customer

If an organisation has a strong purpose that is focused on serving humanity, it may have clarified how it will deal with its customers. Organisations such as Tesco have a huge focus on delivering value to their customer and they do their utmost to deliver products that are the cheapest they can negotiate from their suppliers. However, this has led them to squeezing their suppliers so much that suppliers have then complained that they cannot make a profit by supplying them. This satisfyingly led to customers boycotting Tesco for acting unfairly with their suppliers! Some customers in the UK, at least, are highly sophisticated and do not want to be benefitted at the expense of someone else.

Some utility companies I researched profess to care for their customers and their TV advertisements proclaim that fact. However, multiple, unclear tariffs and unjustifiable rises give the lie to many such utility companies declarations. It has taken strong pressure from Ofgem, the utilities regulator, to require companies to create clear, fair tariffs so that customers can make accurate assessment of which company might best serve them. Companies that profess to respect their customers whilst at the same time ripping them off, fail both the Integrity and Respect test.

It is interesting that during the UK's recession over the last seven years, the John Lewis Partnership and Waitrose have thrived. Of all UK organisations I have researched, they have the strongest customer respect focus. There are other companies less well known who are equally respectful of their staff and who have created company practises that put people first. Madgex is one such organisation.

Case Study – Madgex

It was set up in 2000 by five men who formerly worked in corporate environments and wanted to create a very different type of company. According to their staff, they were laid back guys who had an idea and wanted to run with it. Their idea was to create a flexible company to work for – as they understood that to work was not just about the work-life, but also about your home life. They wanted their staff to be happy — they knew that you take your whole self to work and flexible working was how it worked best for themselves, so it had to be the best for others also.

Madgex has become the market leading supplier of job board software and online recruitment solutions. Wellbeing and happiness at work is at the core of their strategy and with proven results it has seen extremely low staff turnover of 3.7% and external recognition having achieved;

- Investors in People Gold award. Only 1.12% of UK businesses have attained this award.
- Great Place to Work list (2014, 2015)
- N°. 42 in the Best Small & Medium Sized Workplaces in Europe (June 2014)
- Sunday Times Top 100 Best Small Company to work (2009, 2014, 2015)
- Investors in People Health & Wellbeing Good Practice award (2014)
- Simply Health Healthy Workplace Award (February 2014)

With the founders grounding, the HR Director has created an organisational environment of transparency and inclusivity where people are trusted and empowered to work to their full potential. This provides for a happy, engaged workforce. Everyone understands that people have lives outside of work and because they are allowed to be flexible and treated like adults, people want to work for them. Their people want to work hard, because they're engaged and treat the company as their own. They want to stay working for them. There is no hierarchy – they have an open plan office. The CEO is often noted for his approachability and regularly debates challenges with staff. It is a small company –

only 90 staff, but this scenario is played out in many other small companies. These principles however can be replicated in attitudes, styles of behaviour and seating arrangements in larger organisations.

In this same organisation, employees work a 37-hour week, most of the time. When a person is asked to work late, for example to meet delivery schedules to clients, they just take time off at a later date (they just need to communicate with their manager). The policies and people approaches of the company are written to create a humane environment, where people and their private lives are respected. If a person had a family problem to see to, it was understood if they had to leave there and then to take care of it. People are rewarded well with a generous benefits package. Salaries are benchmarked against the size of the company, its industry, against activities the people perform and against their experience and they are paid competitively according to the levels set by external consultants.

Altogether, this makes for a very positive working experience for those people employed by this company. There were other things the leaders of the organisation did that built mutual respect. They have an open, honest atmosphere, with a company meeting every quarter to update everyone in the company about what had been achieved in the previous quarter, which includes details of meeting targets against forecast, strategy updates, clients served, or newly won and a free flow Q&A at the end. They are treated as equals by being included in to the progressive issues of their business and as a result, feel respected and valued.

Respecting The Organisational Intelligence

Leaders who do not respect their employees will not be able to avail themselves of the collective intelligence that sits in their organisation. If you could measure how much intelligence has been bought and paid for in the number of employees that your organisation has employed, and were able to quantify it, it would be huge. Consider how many years of experience, awareness, comparative knowledge and memory is housed in each employee? How much brain power and intelligence can be applied to any problem that a large corporate faces in a situation, issue or challenge? Yet the absence of respect often translates into ignoring the opportunity that this organisational intelligence represents by excluding employees from many of the significant issues and challenges that organisations face.

Yet I see this intelligence at play in business all the time! I am often challenging senior managers and leaders to access that intelligence by inviting their workers to help them address their problems directly. It sometimes appears that executives think that they have very different/special intelligence that enables them to tackle some problems that mere workers cannot! (Perhaps it is this very delusion that enables them to pay themselves such hugely higher salaries.)

On occasions where I have facilitated a leadership team with its middle managers, what becomes evident is that the managers have a very clear awareness of problems that the executives thought were hidden, plus they have accurate assessments of what should be done to correct them. Most business problems are obvious to all, and their solutions are clearer to those lower down in the hierarchy, because they don't have the blind spots that senior people have (who may have even created the problems in the first place)!

ENLIGHTENED LEADERS PERSPECTIVE

Enlightened leaders actively seek for and listen to the individual and collective intelligence of their employees. They can see that it brings the best possible result for the organisation. In order to access it, respect is extended, as it is the key to opening the door. Having Respect allows them to see their employees in a different light, one that recognises their individual value; that gives recognition to the intelligence, experience and talents that can be applied to the organisational problems that need solving.

When respect is at play, communication processes tend to be two-way. Leaders are more open to asking questions of their staff and listening for the wisdom that can come from them. When executives are not respecting their staff, communications tend to be one way – down. When both sides extend respect, there can be a two-way interplay of communication, based on mutual respect and an understanding that different people need to play different roles, with different activities and outputs that are all needed to make an effective, thriving organisation. Two-way communication allows for the intelligence that is gathered from their respective activities to be shared. Problems are shared, allowing for much greater input from a wider range of employees able to shed light on the issue. Sharing the problem enables sharing the solution and the responsibility to take action collectively. This is true engagement.

It is therefore surprising that in many organisations, the leadership team choose to make significant decisions with very little input from their people. Such leaders never doubt that they should! It's as if they have a large blind spot to the fact that there are other people in the world (very close to them) who have answers that may even be better than theirs. Enlightened leaders do not make this mistake, their respect for other people ensures that they ask and they listen to input and help.

Organisations use Engagement Surveys as a way to determine whether the majority of people in their organisation feel that they participate in the running and decision making of the company. The intelligence that is gathered through this means can be extremely valuable. Where senior executives choose to ignore the value of such feedback, it is because they wish to avoid feeling the exposure and any criticism that differing views might represent.

The value of such methods predicates an environment that recognises and respects the intelligence of its people, and wishes to garner their wisdom. Engagement Surveys are effective when the intelligence that is gathered is used in improving the culture, the experience of the organisation's customers and ultimately, the experience of the Executive themselves. At senior levels mutual respect allows for inter-personal challenge, where truth and better solutions than the one brought forward by any one individual can be actively sought.

> *"It is not possible, many argue, to insist on respecting both difference and sameness when it comes to moral values: on having individual and cultural diversity while holding that certain moral values go to the heart of what it means to be human and always have, since the beginning of time, and always must if we are not to lose touch with our humanity. "*

Sissella Bok, 'Common Values'.

By staying in touch with their humanity, enlightened leaders ensure that respect for themselves and others is exercised to draw out differences and to find value in those differences. Respectful leaders value diversity and are interested to listen to alternative perceptions of a situation. They also respect other people's abilities to find solutions they can't and to share responsibilities so that others can make the changes that are needed. By allowing them to do so, Enlightened leaders respect their contribution and the benefits that therefore must be given them.

RESPECT TEST

- What is the quality of our communication processes and do we demonstrate respect to our employees in them?
- How much of our communication processes involve listening?
- How does our company demonstrate respect for our customers?
- How does our company demonstrate respect for our employees?
- Do we respect our suppliers and how do we demonstrate that?
- Are we clear about our fees and charges?
- Are we abusing our position in respect to any part of our supply chain?
- Are we creating win — lose contracts for our employees?

Chapter Seven

JUSTICE/FAIRNESS

Justice to mean: an exacting standard relating to what is just, appropriate or fair when transacting between people or between people and things.

Fairness to mean: an evaluation of balance between a person and the return, reward or recompense that should appropriately be supplied to them as a result of their activity.

Our collective human consciousness is continually evolving in its appreciation of what is fair and right. We who are alive today are in the vanguard of tomorrow's thinking and tomorrow's conscience today. This is very easy to see in the arena of Justice.

The principles that operate today in our work environment, both in the employee contract and the legal contracts that define business relationships, have been created by the intelligence we have applied to the circumstances that we have faced. Our intelligence has formed up the constructs that make up work and the fair or unfair relationships that go to make up our market economy. For example, until computers and mobile technology enabled us to work from anywhere, work used to be turning up to a place, spending time there 'in work' and leaving it at the end of the day. Instead of having a specific place to go to, people can now login and log out of their computers at home, or at the local cafe, and "do their work". The contract of work was fulfilled by employees appearing at the place of work, producing or facilitating some things and going home after 9 hours. The constructs of 'work' are now in a state of flux and former boundaries of work and home have broken down. Many people now do a part of their work at home, on the train or whilst in transit from one place to another. The fairness of contracts is now not so clear.

Humanity in the workplace is a concept whose time has come. In fact, the quality of the workplace has changed drastically. What we would normally do "at work" we can now do with the same quality but in an environment that could be more comfortable, humane and at ease. We have moved out of the Industrial Age and into a more individual and personal, humane environment. Yet there are other parts of our planet, which are paying the price for our great wealth and technological advancement both at the level of planetary plunder, pollution, environmental degradation, dying out of species; and the continuing poverty and desperation of some people who work for pitiful wages to supply us with the products and goods that we enjoy.

During the eighteenth century the law of the U.S. and UK, allowed slavery to exist as a part of commerce. Great wealth was created by slaves for landowners in the southern United States and in the Caribbean for the British. Today, our evolved consciousness of what is just and fair says that it is illegal to take away people's liberties and enforce them to work for the benefit of others. Yet, some large corporations turn a blind eye to the unjust treatment of workers in sweatshops, factories and mining, using child labour and workers on starvation wages, who are producing the products that they will go on to sell at comparably high prices. Nike, Primark, Gap are all cases of such organisations that have faced public outcry about this, but who continue with unjust practises.

In the US particularly (though this mindset has traversed to the UK and other countries) there is a widespread belief that companies have a legal duty to maximise their profits over any duty to employees, suppliers or the community. This mindset was set in motion by the case of **DODGE V. FORD MOTOR COMPANY**, (referenced earlier), a case which is often cited as establishing the principle of "shareholder value" in companies. However, many lawyers have pointed out to me that since then there have been many other cases that weaken this principle in the US, and categorically in the UK, there is a specific item in the Companies Act 2006 that rebalances this one-sided picture.

My thanks to Richard Murphy* for drawing attention to the fact that UK companies have a duty to promote the success of the company for the benefit of all its members; ie., employees, suppliers, customers and to be concerned for the company's impact on the community and environment. This same clause requires directors to promote the success of the company and its members by making decisions with regard to the likely consequences long term. This so little known, that I am including it here in full:

The Companies Act 2006:

Section 172: Duty to promote the success of the company

1. A director of a company must act in the way he considers, in good faith, would be most likely to promote the success of the company for the benefit of its members as a whole, and in doing so have regard (amongst other matters) to—

   a. The likely consequences of any decision in the long term

   b. The interests of the company's employees,

   c. The need to foster the company's business relationships with suppliers, customers and others,

   d. The impact of the company's operations on the community and the environment,

   e. The desirability of the company maintaining a reputation for high standards of business conduct, and

   f. The need to act fairly as between members of the company.

When I first came across this item in my research, I thought – well, here is my case in black and white, written into law. Directors should not be taking decisions to benefit the organisation short term, and should be taking decisions to benefit all stakeholders, not just shareholders and themselves. So, why are these principles not applied? It is a mystery!

In many large corporations there is sometimes (but not always) a General Counsel on the Executive team; a role normally performed by a lawyer and sometimes on the Main Board, in a joint role with the Company Secretary. I have personally coached several such senior executives and it has been interesting that that very few of them have ever felt comfortable or interested to take on the role of 'Policeman' to the

Board. Most often their role focuses on the external world, overseeing the legal functions of buying and selling companies, managing litigation issues and generally protecting the company to do what it has always done (however suspect its practices, or detrimental its impacts). The Company Secretarial role focuses on meeting the regulatory requirements of listing and corporate governance issues. How far the Company Secretary can go in steering decisions in any particular company to ensure compliance to Item 172 is open to speculation. The Company Secretary documents minutes, decisions and lodges the relevant documents to appropriate authorities rather than provide legal advice or counsel.

Whereas I believe it's important that someone competent in the law be involved at a strategic level to advise directors on what is just or fair in joint ventures, international trade, the matters of employing staff, remuneration, benefits, paying and dealing with their suppliers in an ethical and just way and treating their customers fairly. As well as corporate governance issues, corporate social responsibility matters have become more important in the communities in which an organisation operates and calls for a higher level of awareness of justice.

At lower levels, this may be what individual lawyers are doing; but at a strategic level, Justice with a concern for the internal alignment of the organisation towards fairness and justice are overlooked. It seems that instead of this, the General Counsel and their team of lawyers come under pressure to find legal loopholes, and legal justification for doing whatever it is that the Board wants to do. It seems that mostly what Senior Executives want is to make the most amount of money in the quickest and least costly way. The Corporate Social Responsibility agenda is often put into the hands of the HR Director, rather than the General Counsel, who is asked to establish ways to address the company's social responsibilities in the various communities in which it operates; whilst an Ethics and Compliance agenda is sometimes avoided and ignored.

My research into this has identified that of the FTSE 100 only 23 have a legal officer on their board. Of the next tier – the FTSE 250, only 13 have a legal officer on their Board.

The reason I am labouring the issue of General Counsels is to suggest that if Justice is not taken seriously at the Board level by consistent consultation with the General Counsel (who is most likely aligned to Justice), what hope that justice or fairness would have much sway in organisations? This needs correcting, and quickly, if justice and fairness are to be an active component of organisations working in a principled manner.

A recent legal case relating to General Motors highlights the conflict of interest that can arise when lawyers are not advocates of justice, but advocates for their employer. In-house lawyers for General Motors had been defending wrongful death claims from customers for eleven years whilst knowing that the GM vehicles concerned had an ignition flaw that could cause accidents. They didn't report the flaw internally or to regulators because they didn't want to prejudice the company's position in ongoing and future litigation.

General Motors has now acknowledged the ignition flaw which killed 13 people in 54 accidents. If lawyers cannot speak the truth and do what is just, what needs to change?

The penalties that General Motors had to pay in this case was to fire 15 employees, half of whom were in-house lawyers or investigators working for the law department and recall 30 million vehicles at a cost of more than $2.5 billion. No-one has been criminally charged, nor imprisoned for the perpetuation of lies that were propagated for over 11 years. An interesting side note is that General Motor's external legal counsel has not been criticised or punished for the same deceit and the very same behaviours.

Who should be the conscience of the Board, for surely someone needs to be so? Lawyers in the role of General Counsel are seen to be advisors, but rarely is their advice taken if it's in conflict with what the CEO or the majority of the Board want to do. If the Board is composed of individuals who see the purpose of business as making money and delivering value to their shareholders (and thereby achieving the performance measures that rewards them), who should be the voice of justice? Who should provide the moral compass if the Executive Team is moving off course?

It is suggested in some circles that this is the role of the Non-Executive Director, especially if one of the NED's is an accomplished lawyer. However, everything I have been told about the role and actions of Non-Executive Directors is that though they may provide excellent counsel or advice, they are rarely powerful enough to intervene in any meaningful way. Their counsel is seen as advisory, but rarely is their advice taken if it's in direct conflict with what the CEO or Executive team members want.

Who should be the moral compass of the company, if not the General Counsel? Who can provide a neutral, truthful and just alignment to fair ways of dealing with human beings in relationship to the company? When discussing this with a very experienced General Counsel, he suggested that most Board members did have a professional ethic for fairness and justice, though some of the decisions taken by Boards contradicted this view.

Another very senior lawyer of a FTSE company told me of a previous experience where he had overseen the merger of two subsidiaries (both of major international corporations). The two subsidiaries were being brought together in order to (within a short space of time) be floated as a separate company on the Exchange. He observed that the newly constituted Board of the merged company were taking an aggressive approach to getting the new merged company ready for the IPO, which included changing the company policies immediately to enable them to buy Porches, travel first class on trains throughout the UK, whilst not enabling their junior employees to claim for short train journeys between their two offices in the Midlands. Their motivation was clearly personal greed. Was this fair? Was this just? Who should have spoken up to advise them about fairness and justice in this instance? He obviously did not feel it was his duty to do so, or if he did, he believed they would ignore him.

In such circumstance, executive leaders have a clear run at using their authority and power to benefit them at the cost of being unfair to others, whilst contravening their fiduciary duties of taking care of the finances of the company on behalf of the owners.

What about situations when senior executives ignore internal policies with regard to salary benchmarks, roles and benefit packages either for themselves or those they wish to employ? Such overthrows of internal policies and rules are rife in many listed companies. This allows an unjust culture to be created, that then leads to a further perversion of justice and fairness in many subtle ways.

Most companies use an external consultancy benchmark of scales of salaries and benefits related to company size, role and activities performed. They have policies that require everyone responsible for hiring new staff to use these benchmarks when recruiting. In my research, I became aware of some organisations where such policies were patently ignored just because an executive wanted to hire a particular person and they wanted to pay them whatever they thought was appropriate, as well as to load them up with whatever share options they could get in order to persuade them to join. Such disrespect of company policies and rampant egotism in executives promote a flagrant disregard of the law (whether it's internal policies or national company law), breeding a culture of corruption, privilege and entitlement. People, who have been brought into a company by this methodology, feel free to practice this when hiring new people of their own, thus perpetuating the corruption.

There are also power issues between the executive team, where HR directors are frequently ignored or treated as having lesser standing than the CEO and CFO. So instead of a group of independent, equal individuals debating the issues, there are often power plays that discount or invalidate specific people. If senior executives and Board members are composed of individuals who use their position to disregard justice and fairness, who is there to stop them? It is no wonder that enlightened leaders are required, to provide impartial, unbiased perspectives that will generate more just and fair outcomes.

Who in the organisation can be held responsible for such unjust practices happening? It seems that there are not enough checks and balances to the power and decision making processes of Executive Teams and Boards of quoted companies. If not enough attention is paid to fairness and justice at the top of an organisation, corruption and greed can bloom, breeding a similar culture throughout the organisation. There have been many management studies demonstrating that whatever behaviours leaders' role-model will be the behaviours that their subordinates adopt and there is no need to repeat them here.

At first there may not be big injustices, or policy infractions, but often they are the markers of corruption to come and unless leaders and managers are onto these matters quickly they will breed. It is more likely however, that minor cases of stealing of stationery at lower levels of the company will be strongly dealt with, whilst major perversions are overlooked because they are being done by executives.

Who should change it; the HR director, the General Counsel or the Compliance Director? If any of these are not on the Main Board, they don't even get to have a voice, let alone the power to make a difference.

Executive Pay and Privileges

An organisation that practises justice and fairness in its systems of operation can be recognised by examining the employment contracts, rewards and benefits provided to its people. It can also be found in the contracts between itself and the companies/people involved in its supply chain. The justice or injustice of the recompense systems created by the organisation come about when benefits accrue to some of its employees more than others without due reason. It is in this area that executive pay versus the pay for lower level staff and mid-level staff comes into focus. Injustice can also be seen where an organisation tilts its contracts to benefit itself at the expense of its suppliers.

Obviously, a corporation does not have such rules, and operates to make as much profit as possible at each interaction where costs or payments to others can be lowered. Taking advantage of every opportunity to benefit its own bottom line is the norm; whether it's payment to workers in sweatshops of pitiful wages, (whatever remonstrations can be made that wages are fair for that country) suppliers who are squeezed in a variety of ways or farmers who barely make a profit on the sale of their agricultural produce to supermarket chains. And all for what, one might ask? The answer that is mostly given is to pay shareholders more – either through dividends or for the share price to increase. Well, that's the avowed intent, but what it most often means is quite another thing.

The *KPMG Guide to Directors' Remuneration 2013* makes for salutary reading. The median salary levels for chief executives, finance directors and other executive directors in FTSE 100 companies were between £500,000 and £850,000. But when annual bonuses and performance based bonuses are added in, the compensation went up to between £2 million and £3.5 million. The most common performance measure for executives is Total shareholder return, thereby tying in those executives to delivering profit as their primary inducement and for little else. Their salary and bonus package is therefore tied to delivering profits.

On 21 July 2014, the Daily Telegraph published that it now takes the average FTSE boss just two days to earn what the average worker makes in a year. The average FTSE chief executive earns £4.7m; the average UK salary is £26,400. The differential is 178 times greater. How much greater are the productivity and contributions of CEOs and Board members to the success of the company, than those of their managers, or their workers? What validates a differential of 178 times an average worker's salary?

Research conducted by the Incomes Data Services found that FTSE 100 chief executives were paid about 143 times the pay of their average employee, against 47 times the average pay in 1998. This means that salary increases of executives have increased by more than 300 per cent, whilst workers salaries have possibly increased by a minimal factor or even decreased.

Hence, the increasing wealth gap that has become apparent over the last decade.

One wonders how much of the benefits paid out to Directors are actually the monies that more fairly were due to workers lower down the pecking order, or fees payable to suppliers who have not been fairly recompensed? It is this concern that causes many people to feel that injustice has occurred and that they do not have the means to correct the injustice. Those within organisations that have the power to alter this imbalance do not wish to, as they would be the ones to lose by it.

A further significant point with regard to the privileges that executives receive is that they begin to feel that they are entitled to them, and being entitled to them makes they feel that they are better than everyone else who doesn't have those privileges. I know this from personal experience — jetting around the world business class and staying at four and five star hotels makes you feel great! You soon forget that it's someone else paying the bills and you get a swagger in your step and a feeling that this is the life for you. You think that by being in better environments and better class of lifestyle, that this makes you a better person. Which is nonsense, but it's very, very easy to get to that state.

The results of this are that it leads some executives to treat those not sharing these privileges with disrespect and disdain. They disengage with the Humanity Principle of fairness and justice, and never question why they have these benefits and others don't. They perpetuate a self-deception that then becomes part of the communal deception theatre that makes up the culture of their organisation. They go around (in the words of one partner of a national accountancy firm) *"like they're able to walk on water and should be treated with adulation."* They come to believe that they are entitled to better treatment that others aren't. They demote others in their minds, disrespect them and (like the owners of slaves in America's Deep South before slavery was abolished,) believe that some people are lesser and they can abuse them. They may not treat them like their property as slave owners did, but they can certainly demand subservience by people, requiring no challenge or contradiction. Such leaders dehumanise people by relegating them to being an issue of "costs to the business" and cut their jobs when they want to have more profit and more benefits for themselves.

Unenlightened leaders disregard the fact that humans are equal and that equality demands respect and fair treatment. In the book *'Leadership and Self Deception'* the Arbinger Institute provides a powerful detailed dissection of the creation and ramifications of such self-deceptions. Deceptions that I have seen in practise many, many times. It takes a great deal of self-honesty and an adhesion to the principle of Truth to be willing to confront the communal deceptions that Executive Boards manifest and practise as an ongoing mode of operation.

Shareholders could play an important role in re-directing the focus of senior executives beyond benefitting themselves, beyond profit and into a wider delivery of value, into the world, the company's suppliers, and workers in and outside of the company.

Professional shareholders traditionally have had a narrow view of what they want from business investments, which is profits, either through capital growth or dividend payments, but they are also beginning to see the downside of this focus. Norway's Oil Fund and the world's biggest sovereign wealth fund told brokers in 2014 that it was launching a campaign against what it regarded as governance misdemeanours, including groups that combine the top executive top job with that of the Chairman. This is a positive step taken by a powerful shareholder that can hold companies to account. We need more shareholder initiatives that make executive teams accountable not just for financial performance, but for human principles and practises.

Shareholders should re-consider the Performance Measures that Board members are assessed by, and they should include in such matters as employee happiness, employee engagement, delivering value to their supply chain, customer satisfactions or complaints, paying fair wages to third-party labourers, and raising the levels of ethics and justice in their business and legal contracts. It is by this fairer and more just distribution of wealth that commitment and loyalty can be won, and the long term success of the company can be guaranteed.

Justice in The Supply Chain

Economists have identified the modus operandi that guarantees high profits for organisations happen precisely because they can make other people pay for their costs. They have even given it a name —

Externality. What externality means is that you find ways to externalise the costs that currently are borne by workers or systems in your own business and make others carry them. This is now a familiar factor for profit generation – self-check outs at supermarkets, and machines for customers to conduct their financial transactions instead of employees of the business servicing customers is a widespread activity. Ordering and paying online (as well as being charged for the privilege) is another way that businesses externalise their costs upon their customers. Another term for this is really "the science of exploitation" which is a term suggested in the film *'The Corporation'*.

Some examples that are not evident in our everyday lives is how companies externalise their costs by making their suppliers and third party workers bear their costs by under-paying them. Examples of how this works are: Workers in Bangladesh are paid £1 per day for work that would cost £70 for an equivalent employee per day in the UK. UK firms who subcontract their production to workers in Bangladesh are enabling them to subsidise the costs of a British business. Paying people £1 per day is said to be a fair wage, because it is the minimum set by the government. Whether that is a true living wage allowing workers to meet basic needs and to provide some discretionary income is doubtful.

Even in the UK, 'externality' is used by many businesses to make them more profitable, by paying lower wages than they should pay. The BBC in a news article recently identified cleaners being paid the minimum wage of £6.31 per hour to work for two hours work that actually required three –sometimes even four hours. Yet they were only paid for two. The manager of my local Tesco store proudly told me that he regularly works 12 hours a day and is in that store for those 12 hours. I wonder whether the salary he receives from Tesco adequately pays him for his time and work and what that translates to in terms of per hour? This is another way that externality is operating – people working harder than they are paid for, in order to generate profits for the company, from which they may never benefit. Since the economic downturn, many organisations offer the lure of personal advancement, promotion and bonuses if "X" occurs. Whether in fact they deliver the promised promotion or bonus is doubtful. In 2015, it is rumoured that Tesco will have to cut 10,000 people from their staff in order to get back to being profitable. I wonder whether Tesco will remember the loyalty and hard work of my local manager who regularly worked those extra hours and make sure not to fire him?!

In many professional services firms, the feature of people working for greater hours than they are recompensed for has become extreme. Lawyers, accountants, architects, engineering consultancies, all seem to breed a culture where working for far longer hours than people are paid for, is promoted as worthwhile and a ticket for promotion into partnership, or bonus payments. Such advocacy appears more like mental indoctrination, brain washing or coercion depending on the culture of different organisations. Little account is taken of the stress, ill-health or burn-out that may ensue as a result. The impact of such modes of working on individual human beings is often ignored or discounted. This is of course, not true of all such organisations but I wonder how many each reader of this book can identify?

I've worked with many different people in businesses with different cultures and some confirm that there is direct and indirect pressure and role modelling by senior members that's saying to them that they have to work long hours; else there's going to be a personal run-in with the boss or personal criticism of them by the leadership, or that there will be a negative impact at their performance review and on their bonus. It is suggested to them in roundabout ways that other people are working much harder than they are. These kind of subtle threats create a culture that's pressured and unjust and is unlikely to lead to a humane or happy environment. I have experienced it myself at different times within corporate culture.

Mostly people are moral beings, who wish to work hard and honourably meet their commitments. However, if they do extra because they want to, justice would be better served if they were given recognition and praise by their boss or leaders. It is true that often people do more than they are paid for, as their employment contract can never be as detailed as the job that they do and there is an unwritten expectation that people will do the extra bits and pieces that go along with their status and role. As it's not contracted for, people expect (quite rightly in my view), that at the human level, other people nearby/above them, would recognise and recompense them, if only by a "Thank you" or "Well done". Fairness and justice can be served as much by a thank you as a bonus.

If there is larger vision for the business that people can relate to, people will work extra hours because they believe in the mission, because they want to be the best that they can be and because it's fulfilling their personal purpose as well and the organisation gets extra as a result. It would be fair if the organisation were to acknowledge this and give recognition or some benefit as part of the intangible contract between people. The recompense may not need to be money but it does need some acknowledgement. Injustice and abuse comes when people's extra contributions are seen as normal and then required. For justice would say that if a person works 60 hours per week they should be paid for 60 hours per week, which would be fair.

In this situation leaders need to have the awareness and sensitivity to see that they are the representatives of the organisation and therefore need to act on behalf of the organisation to provide recognition or rewards, even if it's only saying 'Thank you'. There is sometimes confusion as to who the leaders are and who can speak on behalf of the organisation. This often leads to middle managers and senior people expecting those above them to provide the 'thank yous', whereas their direct reports see them as the ones they expect the recognition from.

Issues of justice and fairness relate to the fact that often there are two contracts at play. One is the espoused one, the written and signed contract and the other is the one in action, which is not openly discussed or agreed to by the parties involved. For truth and justice to be served would require a leader to step up and say: *"This is the purpose of our organisation, this is our mission. We're going to give you a written contract that says we will pay you to work for 38 hours per week, but actually, honestly and truthfully, the contract we want you to work is 50 hours per week, because only that will enable us to be profitable. If we are profitable, we will share the profits with you."* Saying that openly and giving the person an opportunity to agree or not agree to it, would be fair.

Few leaders would do that openly (probably because they would be taken to court!) because top leaders generally don't work as hard as the people who work for them, and they don't want to share the profits with them. That is closer to the truth, as many corporate executives get paid in excess of what is actually fair and due to them!

Robin Hood Philanthropists

In English myth there is the legend of Robin Hood. He and his merry band of men stole from the rich and gave to the poor. On December 9, 2010, Warren Buffett, Bill Gates, and Facebook CEO Mark Zuckerberg, signed a promise they called the *'Gates-Buffett Giving Pledge'*, in which they promised to donate to charity at least half of their wealth over time, and invited others among the wealthy to follow suit. Others have followed this example.

However, it makes me wonder how much of their wealth has come from investments whose profits were generated through contracts that dealt unfairly with one or more of their stakeholders – whether employees, customers, suppliers, foreign workers or third party suppliers? How much of their profits were due to externality – the salaries and benefits and costs that should have been paid to workers, suppliers or third party suppliers originally squeezed from their fair share of transactions? Profits being generated by lower wages than could have been paid to workers in factories whose conditions led some to suicide? How much more wealthy would employees of their respective companies be, if the profits of their companies were more fairly shared over the lifetime of the company's existence? The greater the profits, the more likely it is that either customers, employees or suppliers (or all of them to some degree) were exploited in order to create them.

Thus in my mind, such billionaires are Robin Hood philanthropists, who may have generated their profits from people poorer than them and now they are giving them back to poor people (though perhaps not in their own countries). Is there some divine justice at work somehow?

Warren Buffett stated that he only paid 19% of his income for 2006 ($48.1 million) in total federal taxes, while his employees paid 33% of theirs, whilst earning a great deal less money. *"How can this be fair?"* Buffett asked, *"How can this be right?"* He added: *"There's class warfare, all right, but it's my class, the rich class, that's making war, and we're winning."*

Such inequality is unjust. This is not making a case for communism however. Nobel Prize Winner Joseph E. Stiglitz in his book *'The Price of Inequality'* convincingly demonstrates that such inequality not only leads to higher crime, health problems, mental illness and reduced life expectancy, but the economic, business and political impacts are widely adverse also. He identifies many hidden subsidies provided by governments to business that distort markets and the 'rules of the game', which *"give an upper hand to those at the top have compounded the problems"*. (P. 216). He makes a startling yet powerful case that inequality is eroding the rule of law, both at a political and business level. He emphasises that *"regulations can work"* and throughout his book he argues that *"we could actually have a more dynamic and more efficient economy and a fairer society"* if regulations were reinforced to create more equal social, economic and business environments.

There are important alignments to establish in an ongoing sense in any business and rather than generate huge profits at the expense of stakeholder relationships, then offsetting them (a little) by charitable giving into communities, leaders could reorganise their drive to profits from a fairer perspective. When billions have been accumulated into a few hands, these individuals realise that a year spent with $100 million of assets is not much different to a year spent with $1billion.

Credit Suisse's American investment bank, will have pay to $2.6 billion in penalties after it admitted that it was guilty in helping US tax cheats for years. Similarly, HSBC has been accused of helping rich individuals avoid paying tax by sheltering their financial assets in Switzerland. Injustice and unfairness practised at a corporate level teaches individuals that they can take advantage of tax laws to shield their wealth from local authorities.

Fines charged to organisations for illegal behaviour are not paid by the individuals involved, nor by the management who were responsible for overseeing them. The organisation has to pay from its revenues and often the individuals involved are excused from any accountability. It's as if the corporation and the limited liability company have been made a tool for criminal behaviour to run rife. A fundamental tenet of justice should be that the wrongdoer should pay the penalty. Without holding individuals to account, we paper over the deep cracks of broken integrity and give permission for such behaviour to continue.

In these cases, shareholders are paying the penalty by receiving lesser dividends, instead of the individuals who committed the illegal acts and the managers who were overseeing them being forced to pay. This kind of injustice may lead to gaining better justice if shareholders could accept accountability for the part they can play in requiring fairer and more even distribution of wealth.

In the movie 'The Corporation' they say "The aircraft of business is doomed to crash." Businesses are not built according to the laws of humanity, but they are subject to the law of human beings: And, like civilisations that have gone before, which have not respected the evolving consciousness of people which has found translation into law, such businesses will become obsolete or destroyed.

ENLIGHTENED LEADERS PERSPECTIVE

John Rawls in *'A Theory of Justice'* (1971) asks the question *"what rules would mankind contract to obey if they were to establish a social order in conditions where none of them could take advantage of their fellows?"* This pre-condition would be at the heart of a fair and just system in our workplaces. Adopting such a mindset would go a great way to developing Enlightened Leaders.

One of the important points that John Rawls makes is that of *"self-interest properly understood"* (p.361). Enlightened leaders who left us the legacy of the John Lewis Partnership, the Arup Group and the Bourneville Trust understood that self-interest "properly understood" means paying attention to everyone else's self-interest – that is, to the common welfare – as a pre-condition for their own ultimate well-being. The principles and rules upon which John Spedan Lewis established the John Lewis Partnership Trust are thoroughly imbued with the idea that the well-being of the partners would be best served if they dealt with their customers, suppliers and communities with Integrity, honesty, and fairness. Today both inside and outside, the organisation *"provides amenities that it believes will be welcome to individual Partners and will promote happiness, a sense of community and the Partnership's reputation."*

Human beings want to do more than what they sign up for at work, because work satisfies and meets a deep human need for meaning and purpose in their life. People want to feel they're making a difference; they want to feel that they are in service and contributing to something greater than themselves. Whether it's the purpose of the organisation or the purpose of their unit or meeting some need of their customers... people want to feel passionate, they want to feel that their life is meaningful and that what they're doing is part of serving a greater purpose or service to others. The population of young people collectively known as Generation Y are demonstrating such mindsets.

We could say that the GenY generation are the leading edge of the mass of our evolving consciousness. They are at the front of a curve that shows us how future men and women will think, not exceptionally, but as the norm. Several studies of these young people in the work place have highlighted the importance to them of meaningful, purposeful work as a requirement to begin. They want work that allows them need to express their innate talents and capabilities, rather than looking for financial reward. Also known as Millennials, students and young professionals have become known as job-hoppers, demonstrating little loyalty to a particular company, sector or career. In talking with traditional, senior leaders, they often frown upon such mobility, assuming that a young person should spend at least five years in a single company before having a right to an opinion.

The leading edge curve however, is bringing new principles, new rules, where fairness and justice is not skewed to the employer. It is not uncommon for young people with promise to weigh their options and think about where else they might best put their talents to use. Organisations' seeking talent will now have to match their expectations, rather than setting and skewing the expectations to suit themselves. An example that comes to mind is Arjun Gupta, curator of the Toronto Hub which has raised over $1 million for the Sick Kids Hospital and built multiple successful companies – demonstrating the curiosity, selflessness and drive that we are seeing in society's young leaders.

Mark Carney, Governor of the Bank of England, in 2014 gave a speech in London called *'Inclusive capitalism: creating a sense of the systemic.'* He remarked that *"we need to recognise the tension between pure free market capitalism, which reinforces the primacy of the individual at the expense of the system, and social capital which requires from individuals a broader sense of responsibility for the system"* that resonates most strongly. Businesses that align to such human needs will prosper in the world going forward.

Fairness and justice should be the watchwords for enlightened leaders to direct businesses to align their internal and external environments, to build the common welfare and share in the well-being that businesses can bring.

Chapter Eight

INTEGRITY

Integrity: behaviours that adhere to a set of ethics, values and principles at mental, emotional and behavioural levels that can be consciously explained.

The meaning above is certainly one way to express what integrity might be. A more enlightened definition might be:

Integrity: An alignment to the natural core constitution of human beings, with a commitment to express the very best qualities of human life; truth, respect, trust, friendship, justice, love and compassion.

The latter is a higher definition, one that asks more of us than purely being consistent to a set of behaviours that we are comfortable with, or a reference to ethics we might conjure up. Integrity in its fullest sense could be said to be true to one's constitutional creation, (as a human, being humane) in the same way as a university is created with a constitution to perform certain duties and actions and is required to adhere to certain ethical standards and behaviours whilst educating its students. A university can be seen to have integrity when it's meeting its constitutional standards and expressing the purpose of its existence.

In the same way, a human being has a constitutional alignment in its creation. By being created, there are certain purposes that it fulfils by its existence (though the precise nature of what these are has been fought over by religions, agnostics and atheists over millennia). In my world view, I would say for a person to have integrity they need to demonstrate behaviours, attitudes and standards that relate to what being humane is (ie., with love, compassion and an alignment to a moral outlook). More precisely, to live close to the alignment of the best of what human beings can be today.

Integrity is generally understood to be a commitment and adherence to a set of standards, ethics and behaviours that are demonstrated consistently over a long period of time. Integrity means whole, integral or 'the same throughout' ie., what is shown on the outside is what is on the inside – with no difference or flaw. If a person or company represents themselves as honest, caring, espousing a set of values which they actually practice consistently and everyone they deal with experiences the same views, behaviours and attitudes, then they have integrity. If they advocate one set of ethics but behave differently to that, they do not have integrity.

For a person to have integrity we assume they have a set of values and beliefs with which they behave congruently. As external observers, we infer that they have those values by virtue of the behaviours that we see them demonstrate; whereas for a person to claim integrity, they must be able to detail their beliefs, values and ethics and be able to state how their behaviour substantiates them. In business, we see examples where someone will claim to have integrity, espousing certain ethical principles, but then behave in ways that are not congruent with the principles they previously claimed. For example, a finance director claims to abide by a principle of equality and suggests that he demonstrates this by sitting in an open plan space with others who work for him; but then consistently keeps everyone waiting who he has an appointment with, sometimes 15 to 30 minutes and doesn't realise he's breaking his integrity.

Sometimes systems and circumstances challenge individuals to have integrity. For example, when a human being can't be humane because they are brought up and live or work in constrained circumstances, are poorly educated and have little choice; where they are treated by others as a commodity to be used for their purposes eg., in slavery, or even in employment in an environment where there is abuse. People who work in industries where there is a lack of ethics, for example, in certain sectors of the finance industry, where money as a commodity seems to have a corrupting influence and besmirches many participants with its toxicity. Such contexts appear to have an overwhelmingly negative influence upon the people caught in their web so that integrity is unknown or unrecognisable.

Recently the new CEO on his appointment to a major UK bank claimed to value integrity and proclaimed that he was going to change the culture to bring back strong ethical values and integrity to the bank. At the traditional bonus time, 18 months later, the Board awarded all staff 20% extra bonus on top of the bonus levels of the previous year, whilst the bank's revenues/profits were down 35% for the year. When this hit the newspapers, the CEO was challenged about this, but he couldn't see the incongruity of it, even when reminded of his original claims. Everyone outside of the banking sector certainly could see the hypocrisy and inappropriateness of it. Such company-wide blind spots of the lack of integrity often can't be seen inside the industry or internal culture within which they operate.

Individual blind spots are created by long-standing behaviours based on assumptions of what is normal in a particular business. Bankers cannot see that bonuses of 20% to 100% of their salary are indecent when in most other businesses bonuses of 2% to 5% are normal, even when excellent profits (apparently!) have occurred. The finance industry is particularly prone to book paper profits which in reality don't materialise. As a result of the economic bailouts of the banks, this particular bad habit became evident, as profits which had previously been booked (and for which people had been paid bonuses) disappeared into virtual reality. Bankers appear unable to comprehend that to pay any bonus when a bank has become bankrupt and has to be bailed out by the government and hence by tax payers is indecent, unfair and unjust. Their response can only be accounted for by self-deception – held in place as a blind spot to excuse poor behaviour, or an innate psychopathy in individuals or the group.

For a person to have integrity, they need self-honesty and not self-deception, which is not something that can easily be assumed. Small self-deceptions are practised by most people (such as in matters of weight, exercise etc.,) but if a person has a great deal of consciousness, they are more aware when they make statements with such deceptions, and will often internally acknowledge it to themselves. People practising self-deception will not be self-conscious, and may sleep-walk their way through work, adopting the prevailing cultural norms of behaviours without question or self-determination. How this happens and how to change it for the better has been well documented by the Arbinger Institute in their publication, *'Leadership & Self Deception'*. It is explained that when a person behaves badly against another person, they evoke reasons why their bad behaviour was justified and build up a case against the other person. Such self-justification allows the person to continue their self-deception and keep themselves closed off from seeing what is true.

Integrity appears in a person when they live congruently between what they believe and how they behave. However, Integrity should not have the broad allowance that most people give it, which most often is 'To be true to oneself'. For being true to your value systems also means being true to your prejudices and judgements, which have been formed by the local indoctrination that you may have received and may not have reviewed or challenged. An extreme, but clear example by which to see this, is where a gangster boss may have a clear distinction between their ethics and loyalty to their family and their behaviour to those from whom they extract protection money; if they hurt or maim those who won't comply with their rules, they will contravene (not just the law) but other humane principles, such as Justice, Fairness or Respect. When

'Being true to yourself' means contravening other humane principles, you cannot be said to have integrity.

Where Integrity is concerned, it means to be the same throughout – to be in alignment with the best Humanity Principles that we can come to today. An example to explain this is to imagine a glass ball that is unchipped, round and intact. Should there be an inner crack or flaw in its construction, then it won't have integrity. In the human sphere this crack could be seen in the UK MPs expenses scandal; on the outside they espoused sound values and apparently behaved in principled ways, but inside, some MPs were at best hypocritical and possibly dishonest. The system and environment in which they operated bred certain norms which facilitated people thinking they could claim for second homes and other benefits/expenses because everyone else was. This was an instance of unconsciousness and sleep-walking into dishonest behaviours.

Integrity is a concept of consistency of actions, values, methods, measures, principles, expectations, and outcomes. Its opposite is hypocrisy – to pretend to be something that one is not. Hypocrisy is the state of falsely claiming to possess virtuous characteristics that one lacks. "Integrity is a personal choice, an uncompromising and predictably consistent commitment to honour moral, ethical, spiritual and artistic values and principles."

A person with integrity behaves consistently with humane values and is true to the model of what a human should be like. This is more easily seen by considering extremes of behaviours. Someone who steals or commits murder cannot be said to have integrity because stealing and murder are not behaviours that are correct for human beings. An individual who acts in these ways is behaving outside the right standards and values of the human model.

Integrity, Context and Behaviours

There have been a number of experiments conducted by social psychologists to determine how people will behave in different contexts and under different environmental pressures. The experiment was the Psychology department of Stanford University where students were selected to be either warders or prisoners in a controlled prison-like environment and were required to play out their roles for several days. Planned for two weeks, the experiment was halted after six days due to the extraordinary humiliation and torture that the 'warders' perpetrated upon their 'prisoners'.

The power of context and environment were demonstrated to be far more powerful than the quality of the individuals' personal characters. Symbols of power, uniforms, clubs, whistles and silvered sun glasses, were used which created a mask hiding individual identities and personal feelings. Prisoners were made to wear a dress with a number on it to which they would then be referred, and a chain on one leg, reminding them of their imprisonment. Warders stepped up their cruelty day by day, dehumanising people, becoming abusive and cruel, causing one prisoner to have a nervous breakdown. Sexual humiliations and punishment of prisoners happened as though they had done something wrong, despite the 'Warders' knowing that they were ordinary students at the University, like them. The Professor conducting the experiment was in the experiment and at no point did he show any disapproval of warders' behaviours, (thereby being interpreted by them as permission to continue). Extreme stress reactions meant that each day one more prisoner had been seriously damaged and had to be released out of the experiment. The net result of the finding was *'Good people can do very bad things given the situation and system in which the situation occurs.'*

Similar experiments by experts have consistently demonstrated that the humane characteristics of the individuals involved can be changed by the environment and circumstances that they find themselves in. What context or environment is being bred in your organisation? What is being allowed or being disapproved of? What dehumanising stereotypes are being encouraged?

The important thing that leaders in organisations often overlook, is the environmental impact of their decisions, taken on the basis of hard measures and facts, rather than the consideration of values, principles or standards. Until, that is, they are the ones being made redundant or let go. They do not consider the mental, emotional or environmental impact upon human beings of their decisions, or the wider ramifications upon their own character and integrity. Mass redundancies and unemployment of individuals are dehumanised under the broad banner of cutting costs and no mind is paid to the pain and suffering that it results at the personal and family level of those concerned. If cutting costs leads to greater profitability, it means increased salaries for executives and they pay a great deal more mind to that.

Management can receive some powerful insights from individuals joining them from other organisations as to the status of their culture and integrity. A unique opportunity occurs when a person takes on a role in a new company. Their experience immersed in a culture with different standards and ethics to the one that they join, enables them to provide a comparative read-out that could be highly beneficial. HR leaders should perhaps consider a 'joining us' interview after a person has been with them for three months to garner such intelligence.

A person's personal integrity may be more subject to the context of their company than themselves and this is why practising the principles is important. One example that highlighted this was when a manager moved from an industrial company with tight ethical standards to a major mining company with much looser standards and ethics. He had strong personal integrity and saw this as an opportunity to make a powerful difference to the company's culture by embedding strong ethical standards into the part of the business he was responsible for. Within three years he had experienced the difficulty of retaining his personal standards in a culture of senior executives who were operating an environment of entitlement, where they earned huge salaries, could hire other people at exorbitant salaries and generally provide benefits, salaries, bonuses and privileges that were far higher than most other FTSE 100 companies, but which they saw were the norm.

Could he have been able to step back three years and remember being in that more controlled industrial company's environment, whose culture was more ethical, he might have seen that the new company's operation was not too dissimilar to a poisonous broth that he was swimming in every day and might have been wary about the infection factor. Over time, he found he couldn't effect the change in others that he had hoped. Instead of him changing the company, the company changed him, so by the end of his time there, the high salary and benefits that had become normal for him, were now out of reach when he was looking for other companies to supply equivalent packages.

Evidence suggests that people's behaviours change to be much more like those around them and that environment is often stronger than personal standards. It doesn't occur to people that their clarity might become warped because of the people they associate with. The greater the number of people believe and act in a certainly way, the more powerful the influence they exert around themselves and thereby cause others to shift their behaviour to theirs. In effect, this is how a culture is created.

This is what losing personal integrity looks like — to behave lesser than one would have allowed oneself to behave in a better context. It's like having a standard of not stealing for most of your life and then moving into an environment where stealing of a certain kind is seen and practised by most people as normal, and you begin to comply and do what everyone else does, you steal. That's when you lose integrity. You could say your standards have become 'corrupted'. You lose integrity by signing up to the standards you previously abhorred and adopt them as your own, without recognising you have done so. In cases like these, 'being true to yourself' is really being true to others around you.

This in essence is the problem that is at the heart of many financial institutions, as well as many multi-national corporations. The environment/culture is rife with standards that are normal to them, but which other organisations consider to be outrageous and abhorrent. A lack of integrity is not recognised because the norm is perverse and corrupted from the higher standard, so that people cannot see an absence of integrity.

If all your working life you have been in a financial services company that operates a particular way – for example in a way that gives no mind to truth, or integrity and only measures and assesses you on how much profit you have generated for the business, (even if you have to commit minor misdemeanours, like agreeing with your pals to set Libor a few basis points higher or lower so you can make some extra profit for your firm) then you will practise fraud and not think it's such a big deal! This is what has happened in many global banks and the organisations that have paid high prices for such behaviours (though penalties for the individuals involved have been almost non-existent). Their staff know no different, behave no different and expect no different, because it is outside of the culture and environment that everyone in the organisation shares.

The Stanford experiment and others like it, lend weight to the view that environment is more powerful than people, and it is that that can be attributed to the widespread corruption and fraud perpetrated by ordinary people, in organisations lacking in integrity.

Do individuals recognise when someone has integrity and when they don't? As long as they themselves are not infected by the same corruption, the evidence is that they do. People are extremely sensitive to whether people are the same as what they represent themselves to be, or whether there are discrepancies between what they say and what they do. Such cracks of integrity are always recognised by people around them. Leaders who don't know this are constantly surprised when this is highlighted to them or when this is recognised in Engagement surveys. Integrity can seem to be behaving in ways that cohere with the web of standards and values that many others adhere to, thereby adding to what people call culture. New people joining an organisation often stand out because they behave in ways different to the organisation's web of standards and new people are more readily able to identify and point out such differences.

The law and legislation is used to define what should be lawful and what is to be deemed unlawful. As a human race we are trying to capture in statutes, laws and governance those features that define our preferred standards and therefore what we are stating are the benchmarks of our integrity. As we evolve in our thinking and our consciousness grows, so we lay down rules that prohibit travelling down some routes that we may have previously travelled (eg., slavery, child labour, apartheid etc.,) which we no longer want to travel and our laws state – 'no more that way'. The trace of our evolution as a people is therefore captured in our legislation, whilst at the individual level our behaviours maintain our integrity to those standards.

The diversity of the law in different countries causes us difficulties when conflicts of standards and behaviours appear. Respect of individuals may be high in one country, with the same levels of rights for men and women, but in other countries the rights of men are held in higher regard and women are disrespected or controlled in ways that don't give them the right to choose to be or do what they wish. This suggests that we cannot have integrity where Justice is not exercised to enforce equality. Where different values are adhered to in respect of gender, integrity means very different things for men and women in such contexts. In some countries girls aren't educated because they are not perceived in the same way as men. The diversity of context means that on a global basis, we have not yet agreed upon how as a people we are "constituted to act in certain ways, behave to certain standards, value certain things and hold certain moral principles" nor have we agreed what those standards, values and moral principles should be. Thus if you are a businessman in Saudi Arabia, Brazil, Australia, the UK or the U.S. integrity will be perceived very differently.

ENLIGHTENED LEADERS PERSPECTIVE

Michael J. Sandel in *'What Money Can't Buy'*, when writing about universities 'selling admission to children of wealthy donors' says, *"the corruption objection is about integrity – the fidelity of an institution to its constitutive ideals"* – raises a significant issue with regards to integrity. It emphasises the idea that integrity is about being true to one's constitution. Professor Sandel points out that in the formation of universities there is the embodiment of certain ideals, "the pursuit of truth, the promotion of scholarly and scientific excellence, the advancement of human teaching and learning, the cultivation of civic virtue" which get 'sold out' if these become corrupted by the wish for and use of money in determining who is admitted and who is not.

For Enlightened Leaders, the question must be 'How true to its constitutive ideals' is your organisation? What purpose is it being true to? For what reason was it created and how closely to its purpose is it being run? Have other agendas become more important? Have other agendas high-jacked Item '172: Duty to promote the success of the company' of the Companies Act?

Enlightened leaders begin with the understanding that as human beings we have an innate, purposeful reason to live, and that there are ways to live and work to which we should be faithful. They are in touch with their own sensibilities and have an innate value system with principles, values and standards to which they can refer.

Philosophers since Aristotle have been debating the issue 'Are we as specie constituted to act in certain ways, behave to certain standards, value certain things and hold certain moral principles?' The evidence says yes. When we do so, we build integrity. However, research suggests that context – whether political, religious, or cultural has a most powerful influence upon how Integrity is interpreted in any local environment. The environment can be a business, a local community, a tribe, or a nation.

The Humanity Principles model details how as a race we are constituted to operate in these ways. It's just that in the business context some organisations and their people seem to have lost their way, diverging from integrity to an ethical path and this has led to such negative outcomes.

Having integrity doesn't mean always having impeccable ethical and moral stances concerning everything. It does mean to have an ongoing, background attunement to what may be right to the ethical standards that apply in your context, with a desire to move towards them, to gain or remain in integrity.

In our journey in life, we are constantly confronted with new dilemmas and difficulties that we haven't faced before. If we are to have integrity, to continue to be true to the ethical or moral positions we have taken, we will observe each confrontation and ask ourselves what is the right, principled view to take concerning this issue? In these moments, we can look for what resonates inside us, to what already has been decided in principle, so that inside and outside can harmonise and stay coherent.

If part of the meaning of Integrity is to be whole, then this is difficult, because we are not yet finished. Every human whilst alive is in a process of growth and change and our permanent condition is one of change. Unlike a bowl which has integrity when it has no flaws or breaks in it, a person during their lifetime is "metaphorically speaking" constantly being broken and re-formed. This happens to us when circumstances cause us to see the world differently, and we throw out old views and adopt new ones; or sometimes by self-chosen or self-decisive choice, hopefully to adopt better and more humane choices or perceptions.

Integrity at the macro level is in transition at this time, awaiting more global uniformity. Within a nation or group of nations (such as the European Union) where many matters are already agreed, integrity at the macro level means meeting the standards, and principles that belong to those agreements. The Ten Principles of the United Nations Compact* are an attempt to establish those benchmarks – relating to Human Rights, Labour, Environment and Anti-Corruption.

It is important to recognise that enlightened leaders introduce innovative thought and actions for others to follow. As we grow, we need to be able to revise the boundaries of what's acceptable and what is not, to establish better standards of behaviours in our workplace. In business, integrity must reassure us that the individuals, teams and systems of our organisation are providing products or services that are truthful, respectful and fair and can be trusted not to have abused any parties on their way to our customer. Not to constrain people to what they should or shouldn't do, but to set higher benchmarks of standards and behaviours available to others. In this way, enlightened leaders create healthier cultures and more humane environments.

INTEGRITY QUESTIONNAIRE

1. What description would you give to integrity?
2. What does integrity mean to you?
3. How do you recognise a person with integrity?
4. How do you recognise a person without integrity?
5. Do you think it is important for a person to have integrity? Why or why not?
6. What is being rewarded in your organisation that adds to or weakens its integrity?
7. What is being disapproved of that adds to or weakens its integrity?
8. Do you think it important for companies to have integrity and how do you recognise those that do?
9. Which companies are you aware of that fail in integrity? What have they done that tells you they're out of integrity?
10. What do leaders do or not do that fails in integrity?
11. How do you think your leaders perform against your personal measures?
12. What context or environment is being bred in your organisation?

Chapter Nine

TRUST

Trust to mean: an expectation of another based on previous agreements or assumed standards with regards to their response, their quality of interaction or the quality of their execution in respect of an action to be undertaken by them.

Trust is a resultant end point of interactions previously experienced with another, which had qualities of truth, respect, fairness and integrity in them. The quality and level of those interactions go to cumulatively build an expectation of further interactions with those qualities.

Trust is built upon reliability, between what is agreed verbally and what is done physically. When two people interact, if there is a verbal agreement on what each will do, and both do what they say they will do, then reliability is built. If reliability continues to be built over several or more inter-actions, then trust is formed. Trust is created when what has been agreed verbally (whether in writing, email or speaking) has translated into action in the manner that was agreed. Trust once created, continues to exist between the parties (this can be individuals or groups) until one party breaks trust by behaviours that are contrary in nature to that previously agreed. Once broken, to re-establish trust requires extra effort and attention to over-write the bad behaviour.

Trust is an intangible quality whose presence, or absence, has significant impact in hard measurable outcomes for individuals, teams and organisations. Trust is an invaluable and vital element of human relationships. In business as in life, trust is like lubricant oil that facilitates activity and soothes the interactions of difference and conflict.

When leaders speak or write about what they intend to do for their organisation, the individuals within that organisation initially respond to their words as a personal promise or agreement. If leaders meet their commitment, employees extend trust. Employees will look thereafter for confirmation of their initial decisions to trust and until a contradiction arises they will continue to trust. However, Trust means more than consistency of behaviour.

A leader in business who is consistently rude or late for meetings does not generate trust – they generate mistrust – however many times they behave in the consistently same manner. Such behaviour leads others to mistrust her/him, which suggests that trust also has a standard as to what good behaviour looks like and behaves like. Poor behaviour, however consistent, demonstrates disrespectful motives; they cause feelings of frustration, anger and impotence in others.

It is surprising how people break trust without giving a thought as to its consequences, for the consequences of breaking trust in the workplace are huge, both at an inter-personal level and in the additional negativity it builds in the culture and environment for all employees in the business.

If trust is not a quality that is sought and valued in the infrastructure of how people are dealt with – not just employees, but how suppliers, external stakeholders and customers are dealt with – there will be breakdowns of humane interactions at that level. If an organisation fails to establish trust with its customers, its revenues will not grow and as an organisation it won't grow large. Trust in its products or services must generate reliable quality experiences for their customers else they won't buy again, or recommend the product to others.

Apple has grown to be the world's largest company because they have created products that people trust will have good functionality and provide a great experience. So much so, that people will queue up to buy a product they haven't seen or touched yet, merely because it has been made by Apple. There is so much an organisation can do to build trust.

A personal example — I bought an early iPod which I enjoyed but after eighteen months it had some kind of breakdown. When I took it to an Apple store to be repaired, it was sent away and a new iPod was returned, which had four times the memory capacity, greater functionality and a radio and clock. I was not asked to pay anything. For me, this was great service and a great experience. Now I trust that if I have a problem with an Apple product, I will receive not just appropriate service or assistance, I will receive more than I might anticipate. This kind of experience builds exponential trust for present customers but also creates additional ones super-fast.

Compare this to the experience of a retired paramedic with his gas utility supplier. Reported on Mail Online on 22 August 2014, the supplier apparently hounded this man for seven years to pay a bill for a gas supply that he never had. They insisted that he owed them money, (just over £1000) despite him providing evidence to the contrary, threatened him with legal action and then after admitting they had been in error, refused to apologise and offered a risible sum of £50 as a goodwill gesture for the letters, phone calls and distress they had caused.

This kind of behaviour will undoubtedly break down trust. Not only will customers choose not to use such a supplier again, but many other readers of the Mail Online will have had their trust eroded and the reputation of the whole organisation will suffer. In our globally connected world, broken trust with one or a few customers can quickly translate into reputational damage with losses of millions of pounds.

The ramifications of broken trust are huge and barely calculable. A customer who is abused in a derogatory manner will never use the organisation again. Their family members will not use the organisation's services. Each one of them will be passing on the negative experience and with our digital world this may be to thousands of people. Employees within a company which delivers bad customer experiences, who are required to pursue unreasonable claims, and do so by direction of their managers, will lose trust in their managers. The ripple effect of broken trust within and outside of the organisation is wide and ongoing. It is a common saying in business that a person happy with your product or service will tell 10 people. A person unhappy with your product or service will tell 100 people of your failures. Tarnished reputations of broken trust lead to poor company performance and often to ultimate failure, as financial losses can mount up.

How to Build Trust

Here is a simple approach to build a culture of trust in your organization using a three-tiered commitment to a few core trust principles:

1. **Capability trust**, means trusting others and their capability, thus allowing them to make decisions on their own, involving them in discussions, and trusting that their opinions and input will be useful.

Trust in a person is more than trusting that person's character; it is also about trusting an individual's competence and capability demonstrated over time. Trust encompasses the idea that each person is unique, with different strengths and weaknesses, talents and capabilities with manifold different human characteristics. Trust can be applied to a person with respect to their genuineness, but not every person can be trusted to have a particular competence or to deliver a particular thing, eg., a great report, or a great presentation. This is where the unique competences of people need to be more accurately understood and valued for their differences. A person may be trustworthy as a character, but if you needed an appendix to be removed, you would only trust a surgeon with that particular expertise to operate upon you. You might trust a friend with an errand to buy you something and give them £200 but you may not trust them to make a good politician. There is a great distinction between the character component of a person and the specific competence capability they have against a task or activity.

2. **Contractual trust** means meeting consistently and reliably all the terms and conditions of the contracts, written or implied between you and your staff and customers; and delivering to the standards of previously agreed-to expectations.

It is in your interest as a person and as an organisation to build in reliability and trust into your interactions with customers. These can either build or erode trust. I observed an incident on a train, where a young woman handed her train ticket to a ticket inspector who was checking tickets. The inspector said she hadn't validated it by writing the day's date on it, so he confiscated the ticket, and on top of that, then charged her for another one. When challenged for his action (by bystanders somewhat amazed by this double-charging,) the inspector said that these were his instructions and it was all in the small print of the tickets. The kind of attitude demonstrated by the ticket inspector (no doubt well trained by the company), that the person is attempting to defraud the company, rather than making a genuine error, breaks down trust. Their retaliatory action of taking away her ticket and making her pay for another actually was them defrauding her! The company failed to extend trust and lost trust instead. The passengers observing this incident were outraged and discussed how differently other transport authorities approach similar scenarios, thus spreading the comparison of the lack of trustworthiness of that particular train operator.

3. **Communication trust**, means being open with all that needs to be known, by sharing information, providing constructive feedback and speaking with good purpose about people; being proactive to feed through honest and regular information to all who should know. It also invites up-ward flows of communication and ensures there are systems in place to facilitate this.

Leaders demonstrate trust when views different from theirs can be expressed in their presence and can be seen to be valued. Respectful leaders value diversity and are interested to listen to alternative perceptions of a situation. Enlightened leaders value two way flows of communication.

By asking questions (of the kind detailed at the end of this chapter) and engaging in conversations with members of their organisation which includes people from different levels of their organisation, executives might not find it too difficult to identify the changes they need to make to improve trust levels. If leaders reflected upon the nature and quality of trust that they generate or extend to others, they might more honestly assess how they can responsibly add to, or take away, trust from their relationships. They might then introduce some checks and balances to measure the quality of trust that then is engendered and over time improve it.

As noted American writer and journalist Ernest Hemingway famously said, "The best way to find out if you can trust somebody is to trust them." It is important to give people the benefit of your trust first, to extend trust as a starting point and benchmark of any relationship, but if your trust is not met, then you know that greater clarity is required at the contractual level, and a degree of protection is required. Don't wait for someone to prove that they can be trusted before you trust. This is a crucial key for all leaders who are trusted – they trust employees first, and this trust is reciprocated. The reverse is often true – if you don't trust, you won't be trusted.

When trust exists between employees and management and this trust is conveyed to your customers and your suppliers, your business will thrive. Trust creates a virtuous circle that draws in commitment, loyalty and support.

As mentioned previously, Russell Mokhiber compiled a listing of the Top 100 Corporate Criminals of the Decade in the 1990's. The following quotes highlight how the lack of truth and justice in US leaders during this time broke trust between employees and their senior leaders.

> *"So on the one hand, the list shows the pervasiveness of the problem. On the other hand, it shows that there's really a problem of insufficient sanctions and punishment for corporations. Then finally, there's good reason to believe that the list itself, massively underestimates the extent of corporate crime. That's in part because many things that corporations do that*

> *should be crimes aren't defined as crimes,*
> *and it's also because the corporate criminal*
> *police are vastly underfunded and*
> *inadequately equipped to go after the*
> *corporate criminals."*

What the List Tells Us,
Robert Weissman, Editor, Multinational Monitor*

How many organisations currently trusted, should not be? If the publicly listed companies of the world were to do an audit today, to identify whether their organisation **should** be trusted, would they find that they genuinely should or should not be? The case more often, is that organisations want to do as little as they can get away with, not to be found at fault, rather than to do all that they should do, to be trustworthy.

The following quote was made in relation to the United States, but it is just as applicable to the UK or any other developed nation: Marc Barry, Competitive Intelligence Professional*

> *"the 80's and 90's taught American*
> *workers are that, you know, essentially*
> *they're expendable. And, you know, if it*
> *comes down to the CEO of a major*
> *corporation getting a raise, and this guy*
> *getting a pink slip, well, this guy's going to*
> *get a pink slip. So companies' employees*
> *know that their companies don't have any*
> *loyalty to them, and so therefore they don't*
> *have any loyalty to the company."*

The above comments suggest that as potential customers of some companies, instead of trust, we should be on active watch for their criminality, rather than their trustworthiness! Which unfortunately is how many of us are living our lives – mistrust first, then check before trusting, creating a climate of wariness and suspicion.

If an organisation has trustworthy products but fails to provide trustworthy services in conjunction with the products, then customers' trust can be compromised, affecting the way they see the brand and the whole organisation. If an organisation breaks trust with its customers (after it had established it with them) then revenues and profits will undoubtedly fall. "Mistrust doubles the cost of doing business" says Professor John Whitney of Columbia Business School.

Ray Anderson, CEO of Interface Inc., in the movie *'The Corporation** said *"If our words get ahead of our deeds, we risk breaching that trust, so we have to be very careful to avoid greenwash, talking about it but not doing it, or claiming more than we're doing."*

The utility companies of the UK provide a trustworthy product in the form of gas, electricity and water, but some companies' service in providing unclear tariffs and billing and their slowness in dealing with transfers or enquiries has led to many people distrusting their promises. The Ofgem authority in the UK has a number of open investigations into misleading promises made by some of the utility companies and has fined a number of them on cases where their investigations have proven mis-selling, or misrepresenting services. There are even concerns about collusion and price fixing, leading Ofgem to request a market investigation by the Competition and Markets Authority.

Steven M.R. Covey in his book *"The Speed of Trust"** details a powerful argument that when trust is high, speed goes up and costs go down. He references how Warren Buffett completed an acquisition of McLane Distribution (a $23 billion company) from Wal-Mart. A normal acquisition process would have involved six months of due diligence involving accountants, auditors and lawyers. But, because there was high trust between both parties, the deal was made with one two-hour meeting and completed within a month of agreement. In a management letter accompanying Berkshire Hathaway's annual report, Warren Buffett wrote *"We did no 'due diligence'. We knew everything would be exactly as Wal-Mart said it would be – and it was."*

There are many more examples of the correlation between the lack of trust costing far more in time and money, whilst trust operates to speed up and lower costs when two parties have established trust between them.

Trust in Humanity

Trust is extended to you by others when they recognise that as a human you have integrity, you are just and fair, have self-respect, practice respect of others and that you value and speak the truth. When those platforms exist, it's a short journey to be trusted.

All successful companies internally run on trust and loyalty, both ways – from managers and leaders to workers and from workers to their managers and leaders. Bringing forth the best of people in work depends on extending trust and granting autonomy, whilst relying on the human intelligence of the individuals and groups that work together. The pinnacle of business processes that recognises this is called the 'Japanese production system' which trusts the goodwill and creativity of workers and gives them considerable control of their production line. They are encouraged to make suggestions for improvements and their suggestions are acted upon, helping their companies achieve production efficiency and quality so that many non-Japanese companies are now imitating them.

Ha-Joon Chang's quote of the Kobe steel manager in his book *'23 Things They Don't Tell You About Capitalism'* who said, *"You simply cannot run a large bureaucratic organisation, be it Kobe Steel or your government, if you assume that everyone is out for himself"*, affirms how trust in some organisations is inherent in how things are done. Such trust builds trust and grows trust with every interaction, speeding up efficiency, effectiveness and well-being.

If organisations would look at their bottom line revenues and profits and determined how many of those profits were generated because of customer satisfaction, loyalty and trust, they might respect their customers more, and be rather more careful about abusing or exploiting them. They would understand that there is a direct correlation between trustworthiness and the economic impact on their organisation and its place in the market.

Identifying the Characteristics of High and Low Trust

In our workshops on Trust, participants are often surprised by the consistency of awareness amongst large numbers of people of the same things – who is trustworthy and who is not; the character traits, behaviours and credibility of people they all know; who may be trusted for what and who may not be; who may be trusted to sustain trust amongst employees, clients and stakeholders.

There is a consistency of responses to questionnaires regarding current trust levels within their team, their bosses and regarding which other teams may be trusted and which may not be. It is often surprising to us, to see how much is known (however subconsciously) by people who have not had opportunities to collude over answers. It is also evident that bosses who do not extend trust to employees are by return, not trusted.

It takes workshop participants several hours in conversation about trust to understand how their personal behaviours link to a wider group impact on levels of trust in the organisation. It is a surprise to them to see that what they believe are small indiscretions or loose behaviours will be interpreted by others as significant indicators that add to or take away trust. This demonstrates how sensitive and aware people are when it comes to issues of trust.

When we ask groups to identify the characteristics of an organization with high trust, they are quick to note what these characteristics are and they often find agreement on specific organizations which demonstrate trustworthy qualities. When we ask them to identify the characteristics of low trust organizations, similarly, examples are quickly thought of and agreed on.

When as a third step we ask them to examine their own organization against the characteristics they themselves have identified as high or low trust, they quickly have insights on the standing of their company in comparison. Sometimes this is a shock. Very clearly they see what their top leadership are doing to create the high or low trust standing of their organisation. Sometimes they can even see what they are doing! Which powerfully demonstrates the power they have (or don't have if it's their executives' actions) to make a difference.

Executives should examine the costs of lost trust and take time to understand how trust is created, how it becomes established and what activities will lead to it being broken. Trust once broken may be re-gained, and re-built, but only with conscious decisions and definite actions by those who caused the breakdown of trust in the first place. We can all identify organisations that have lost huge market value when their share price falls due to reputational trust being broken. As I write this, Tesco had billions wiped off its share price when it announced that it had over-stated its accounts by £250 million pounds in a business quarter. Volkswagen lost 30% of its value in the first week of the scandal relating to its emission levels. FTSE 100 companies are trusted to be truthful in their statements of accounts to the market-place. When they demonstrate that they cannot be so trusted, the reputational damage translates into economic cost.

The matter that restricts most organisations' ability to confront this issuer is leaders avoiding looking at how the organisation that they lead might be perceived by others, whether by its employees or by customers. Leaders identify themselves with the organisation so they don't want to hear that it is not trusted, as it will mean they are not trusted; so they avoid looking to know and therefore change.

Breakdowns of Trust

The long list of penalties extracted from banks by regulators over the last 5 years is a testament to the cultural nature of the misconducts. The details highlight the global nature of the collusion and range of criminality:

$9 billion was paid in May 2014 by BNP Paribas for violating US economic sanctions against Sudan, Iran and Cuba. HSBC was to pay US authorities $1.9bn (£1.2bn) in a settlement over money laundering and paid $4.2bn for fines and mis-selling in 2012. $1.7bn was paid to cover the cost of mis-selling payment protection insurance (PPI) to mortgage borrowers, bringing the total provisioning for PPI claims to $2.4bn, as well as $598m for mis-selling interest rate swaps to small businesses. The American investment bank of Credit Suisse, will pay $2.6 billion in penalties. Each new fine, like France's BNP Paribas' US$8.9 billion penalty, sets a new, ignominious record. Governments fear that a criminal conviction and closure of a major bank would prove far too disruptive to the financial system, hence are weak in punishing bad behaviours. Big banks are not making significant progress towards changing the underlying business culture that allows these violations to occur and they are being allowed to continue without regulatory changes to force them to make such changes.

Swiss bank UBS, admitted to a key role in the biggest antitrust/price-fixing case in history, the so-called LIBOR scandal, a massive interest-rate rigging conspiracy involving hundreds of trillions of dollars in financial products. It was fined $1.5 billion for this. Many of the world's biggest banks, including UBS, Britain's Barclays and the Royal Bank of Scotland, were also involved and secretly conspired to manipulate the London Interbank Offered Rate, or LIBOR, which measures the rate at which banks lend to each other. In many cases, the misdeeds were committed more or less openly, in writing, with traders and brokers baldly offering bribes in texts and e-mails with an obvious lack of concern for punishment that later, sadly, proved justified.

The UBS settlement demonstrated, without a doubt, that the LIBOR scandal involved more than just one or two banks, and probably involved hundreds of people at many of the world's largest and most prestigious financial institutions – in other words, a truly epic case of anti-competitive collusion that calls into question whether the world's biggest banks are innovating a new, not-entirely capitalist form of high finance.

Additionally, UBS may have to pay $8 billion in fines to settle a probe into rigged currency markets. Interacting with some of the world's largest and most prestigious banks -who similarly committed fraud – their collective action has undermined the integrity of the competitive system. Germany's Deutsche Bank and US Citigroup could face more than $4 billion in fines for their fraud in the currency markets. Whilst JPMorgan Chase paid more than $13 billion to settle charges that it overstated the creditworthiness of securities that contributed to the housing crisis. The bank didn't admit or deny any wrongdoing; though how can paying such a fine be construed as them not doing anything wrong? Mitch Feierstein in his book *'Planet Ponzi'* fiercely advocates jail time for individuals involved in such misdeeds, as well as recognising that it's *"Time to challenge Wall Street's way of doing business, to reject it as unethical – to name it as morally and financially bankrupt."*

In the face of all this, is it surprising that banks are now no longer trusted? Where integrity has become corruption, trust is unjustified and mistrust, suspicion and wariness must take its place. Even though I have provided perhaps too much information relating to banks, there are other industries that have come under regulatory scrutiny and have been fined for bad behaviours. To the lawyers and compliance officers of institutions who exist to control criminality, such corporate wrong-doing must be found and dealt with to the strongest extent of the law. Where the law is still not strong enough to bring to justice those individuals caught in mal-practise, the law must change. Or, perhaps we should apply a rule formulated by Mitch Feierstein in his book *Planet Ponzi "I'd like to see a rule whereby anyone who has earned more than, say five million bucks from a firm would have their personal assets placed at risk if the firm failed due to their incompetence, or following losses incurred when they were at the helm."* This might help!

In the Humanity Principles model, Trust is the end point of the positive cycle. When experiences between people are constructive, trust is created. When the humanity principles have been adhered to, the resulting content lodged in people is trust. Distrust can just as easily be the outcome for people, based on their experience of people or organisation's behaviours. When distrust has been made active in the collective psyche of a group of people, it will take a great deal of work by the organisation or person, in the prior principles – truth, respect, fairness and justice to build integrity – before trust is won again. Trust is the barometer of the practise of the principles.

The Top Four Reasons Why Leaders Are Not Trusted

In business contexts, many engagement surveys identify how employees do not trust their 'leaders', whilst their direct managers are trusted more. In my work with large and medium sized businesses, there are often very good reasons why leaders are not trusted. Employees in HR departments are often not brave enough to point these reasons out to their leaders, so I shall do so here.

Firstly, let me say that I am speaking about leaders in other organisations, and not yours. Let's speak the truth here and detail the top four reasons why leaders are not trusted, and why they should not be!

They lack integrity

Leaders in this category may advocate and may be heard to advocate values, morals or ethics that are worthy, but their behaviours are not congruent with what they say. There is a disconnect between what they say and what they do, and these are cracks in their integrity, which are clearly seen by their employees. These cracks may be flaws in either their competence or their character. Employees are generally intelligent and aware and they know if they are being fed lies, bias, or half versions of the truth.

They are arrogant and disrespectful

Arrogance is often found in leaders with strong ambition who have achieved senior leadership and now look down on others who have not achieved so much. Instead of class distinction, this work distinction causes leaders see their time as more important and keep others waiting, cancelling their appointments or ignoring them if they pass them by. They disrespect others by not allowing them much time to speak; they don't listen to others, take note of what they say or include others contributions into their decision making.

They don't like to hear the truth

Leaders who do not have emotional self-control and permit themselves emotional outbursts, or behave unpredictably, aren't trusted to be consistent and reliable. Employees in fear of their boss having a 'hissy' fit or losing it, will not feel safe to speak the truth to them, and quite rightly will not trust them to be understanding or supportive when they actually need their help. Admitting vulnerability to someone who may respond in widely divergent ways is unsafe and unlikely to occur. This ensures that leaders do not get to hear all that they need to hear in order to make appropriate decisions and their ability to help, or sort problems out becomes seriously hindered. Leaders need to know that this is a situation they are creating, not one that their employees are creating.

They are unfair, unjust and use their power to benefit themselves

The benefits, salaries and bonuses that are paid to leaders are often unbelievable and so distorted against the comparative values of their employees, that in employee's eyes they cannot be justified. Self-serving actions are hidden or not spoken about openly, but if information leaks out, it will certainly be commented upon by employees. They quite rightly do not trust their leaders to not pay themselves excessively, as they demonstrate year after year that they do! The use of such power is apparently delegated to Remuneration committees, but collusion amongst those sitting around the top table to share in the benefits, leads to the creation of a culture of entitlement that is not trusted.

ENLIGHTENED LEADERS PERSPECTIVE

Enlightened leaders recognise the value of building a culture of trust. They work at creating trust between employees and managers, and between managers and leaders. They address how trust is built between the organization and its customers. Solid relationships are built up over time through consistent, trustworthy transactions. They ensure that supplier contracts are fair and just and that their stakeholders feel considered. They measure and review where lack of trust is evident (unhappy customers, unhappy suppliers, disaffected employees, lost business), and take prompt action to rectify the problem.

Enlightened leaders develop an organization with a high cultural level of trust by being clear on the purpose of their organisation and building in principles throughout their people, systems and processes based on truth, respect, justice and fairness and which will lead to behaviours of integrity. If all these principles have been well introduced and abided by, trust will be a natural resultant. If trust is not present, enlightened leaders will identify this as a key warning sign that one of the principles is not operative. By examining the side effects detailed in the respective chapters, they can identify what is out of balance and take actions to correct it.

If trust doesn't come naturally, leaders need to extend trust. Internally with peers and employees, you have to be able to let go of anxieties and trust your direct reports and peers to do what they have to do, without worrying about performance or being in control. Openness and transparency are vital to forming and maintaining trust. Speaking the truth and inviting truthful and open communications between parties is very important to forming real relationships between people. If people cannot be truthful when things are not right, or something is going badly, then honest conversations cannot be had, and trust will break down. Openness means not keeping secrets or trying to hide something from others.

For trust success as an organisation, enlightened leaders recognise and communicate to their employees that they're not in business solely to make money, but to deliver your unique value/contribution and to help your customers. If your employees are facilitated to be customer focused, they can form relationships with collaborative qualities that combine to reach solutions and benefits that are better than either party working on their own and that meet the needs of both. The combined intelligence of both parties — your employees and their customers — will generate trust and deliver better financial results as a natural benefit.

Building relationships based on trust with your customers calls for a very specific focus by your people and teams; having a highly competitive culture driven to deliver profits as the primary success measure and driver, will act counter to this. Trust allows employees to think of their customers and their relationships with them as important over the long term. Employees, who are going to be measured by the new business they win or the sales they deliver in the short term, will find it hard to generate behaviours that will build relationships over the long term. Hence, they will fail to build either deep or long-term trust. Money is a by-product of the successful delivery of value, not the other way around.

Success means taking a long term perspective with regards to the relationships you are forming. In organisational terms this means being aware that you are building your Brand Trust and this will be formed by consistent, reliable delivery on promises made. You are building client relationships that may last beyond the current incumbents in a business. You need to be thinking about your business in terms of long-term relationships and not immediate transactions. Most sales models are inherently transactional, with a lead and a close. Teams and organisations need to think about their business with a medium— to long-term perspective, as an ongoing, ever-flowing cycle, based on relationships of trust, allowing customers to keep coming back.

Trust is a major factor of successful relationships and successful organizations. It is as easy to build trust as to build distrust, where the ramifications are as positive on the up side where trust is present, as they are negative on the downside, where there is distrust. The need to cultivate solid relationships is vital not only for success but survival. Business cycles are becoming shorter and shorter as change expedites competition and customer needs evolve. In the UK, mega retail stores were once preferred, now, customers prefer smaller, less overwhelming experiences. Organisations in touch with their trusted customers gain early insights into such changes and can adapt quickly.

Organisations are facing some of the biggest challenges of the last 50 years thanks to the economic climate of the past few years. Now, organisations are confronting how many of the business relationships they'd previously established are there to support them in the critical times. Thinking and planning for the long term are vital ingredients to building a culture in which relationships and trust can thrive.

TRUST SURVEY

Some of the questions that company leaders can use to conduct an internal investigation on trust levels within their executive team, their employees and with their customers are:

- What are the characteristics of an organization with high trust?
- What happens in a high trust organization?
- What are high trust behaviours?
- What are the characteristics of our own organization?
- As leaders of the organization, are we trusted by our employees, customers, shareholders, local community?
- Are we trustworthy and should they trust us and for what?
- What are we doing or being, to build trust for our organization?
- What behaviours do we admire in other organisations which are highly trusted?
- What are the high trust outcomes for those organizations?
- As an executive team do we extend trust to our staff and are we building a culture of trust?
- Do our customers trust us?
- What measures of trust have we established to determine how and for what our customers trust us?

Chapter Ten

POWER

*Power to mean: The energy and
courage accessible by a human being which
they can take the responsibility to use and
available to exercise on a moment by
moment basis.*

Power sits at the heart of the Humanity Principles model because it is by the exertion of personal power that the Principles are exercised by people, and where they don't exercise that power, negative outcomes can appear. For power to be used a person must also exercise courage, to take accountability for the outcomes that will come from their actions and to deal with them responsibly.

Personal power

Each human has power – the power that is innate in the intelligence, station and standing of being a human being — with all the individual talents and capabilities that nature has endowed us. Our capabilities and the extent that we can use them with regard to our power are enormous. If we look at the manifold things that different people have accomplished, it is huge. Anything one human has accomplished can be done by any other human, though they may not want to.

It is in every person's power to do what Mother Theresa has done, or Alan Sugar, or Richard Branson. Any person may become a doctor, a scientist, or a researcher. The power of being able to accomplish any of these things is available to every individual, though their desire to do so may not be which would constrain their access to the energy to achieve it. However, if the desire were there, the resulting accomplishment will be different, as it's constrained by their education, situation and circumstance. The power of each person is great, but the quality of what they achieve will be coloured by a large range of factors, (some internal and some external), including their personal interest, desire, finances, external circumstance, exposure and education.

Each of us has the power of free will and the choice of how, when and where to exercise our free will. We have the power of choice in every moment, of every minute, of every day. Our choices are manifold, from choosing what we choose to think, to choosing whether we will be self-determining or the victim of whatever family, background or experience we have had.

Each person living has exactly the same power — the power that belongs to a human being – and the human rights that attach to that. That is what the founding fathers of America wished to embody in their Declaration of Independence. *"We hold these truths to be self-evident, that all men are created equal, that they are endowed by their Creator with certain unalienable Rights, that among these are Life, Liberty and the Pursuit of Happiness."*

Even though the power of any person alive is exactly the same, the circumstances in which they live can give them the impression of having less or more power in that they gain more or less access to positive experiences, learning, schooling, tools with which to play, and breadth of exposure to different things. A child being brought up by parents able to send them to private schools where they live in term time and go on school excursions to different countries, will experience their sense of power very differently to children brought up in a village in Cyprus who live at home and don't get taken on school excursion outside their small country. The narrower the experience, the more a person's awareness of their power is limited by what they know and can do, as well as what those around them know and can do. The narrowness of exposure creates restrictions of awareness, not necessarily limitation of power. It takes exposure – such as to the digital and communication revolution over the last fifty years — to dramatically change people's awareness of what is possible, in using their power.

A person brought up in poverty in a third world country may gain the impression that their power is restricted by their access to learning, relating to the world and what they can do it in. If raised in an environment close to nature with awareness of the intuitive range of human abilities, they can get the sense of being greatly powerful, but in abilities the western world doesn't understand.

An example to illustrate this is Nelson Mandela. Even though he was born in South Africa and to western eyes brought up in rural poverty, he was raised at his uncle's court where he was very well educated in the ethical considerations of human values, such as respect, truth and justice. This foundational education allowed him to exercise his power in later life to put him into the vanguard of human rights advocacy. Some people live with the lie that they are weak and powerless, when the truth is that as human beings we are inherently powerful ie., full of power. Each person can make the journey to see that, acknowledge that and own that in their own lives. Our earliest experience as a child arriving here is that we are powerful and as William Wordsworth expressed it *"trailing clouds of glory do we come"*.

Power in The Business Context

When it comes to business, each company organises its people in ways that either enhances an individual's power and enables them to exercise it, or, it selectively confines and restricts people to different amounts of power, in relation to what the organisation wants them to do. For an organisation has a 'Wand of Authority' that it uses to assign people to delineated roles and then grants them certain units of power to exercise in those roles. The power units per Wand are mostly defined by the granting authority, often the CEO, the Board, or HR who grant wands of power to different individuals across and up and down the organisation.

The greater the hierarchy, the more the power in an organisation is tiered and broken up into smaller and smaller units allocated to different people. This normally means that roles are specifically defined and power is granted to each role and limited to the duties required of them. In this way, power is awarded to the role, not the person. However, this isn't always how individuals who inhabit the role understand it, or how they behave whilst in it. False perceptions relating to personal power comes when people confuse the power of the role with their personal power.

The use of delegated power within a business quickly demonstrates whether this is an enlightened leader using that wand or a leader prosecuting more personal agendas. Enlightened leaders use their power to engage others, consult and collaborate; to draw the collective intelligence into decisions that will benefit the whole, they delegate power and control to appropriate levels empowering those responsible to take decisions. They accept policies that control themselves and their peers, which make them accountable to not just their shareholders, but to their employees and their customers. Power with accountability is an excellent partnership.

Un-enlightened leaders use their power in ways characterised as 'egocentric selfishness', by using their position to gain privileges and benefits. When such leaders leave powerful roles and become unemployed, they often feel dramatically lessened in power, which they are, because the power they exercised at work was delegated power. It is then that they feel their humanity and the vulnerability that comes with it. Power within organisations is focused on the tasks and actions that deliver revenues, often denying people's humanity and ignoring the health and well-being of its people. Senior unemployed leaders have to confront the lack of well-being that comes from not having power to exercise, when they are just another person with the same level of power as everyone else.

Power Games

This leads us to the consideration of Power battles which define how power is exercised or abused within an organisation. For some, power is welcomed when they can see what they can do with that power — make decisions, have control, have authority over others, have privileges and benefits others don't have. For those without Wands of authority, power can seem to be 'the right to abuse people' 'becoming the scapegoat' 'being the person to blame for things going wrong' and they avoid taking up whatever amount of power they may be entitled to.

Business leaders sometimes say that they want to 'empower' their team, but some individuals apparently don't want to be empowered, they would rather be told what to do. A client will complain that their staff won't think for themselves, that they come to them for them to solve problems rather than do it themselves. By enquiring more deeply about the context of these comments, what often becomes clear is that the situation has actually been fostered and encouraged by them, because their ego is stroked and their sense of power is increased when those working for them, look to them for answers and see them as the expert.

Collusions form between the senior person and their team to play out these power games. One might ask how and why might this happen? It is obvious what the senior person gets from such power games, but why on earth would junior people engage in this collusion?

My research suggests that by complying in such games, the more junior person gives up their power to think for themselves, work out solutions to problems for themselves and generally not do any kind of thinking for themselves. In return for this, they get the favour of the person above them who enjoys the ego enhancement they get when the more junior person seeks their help. The junior person gets to opt out of the responsibility that belongs with owning the power that belongs to their functional role. They devolve that responsibility to the more senior person. They get, as I often hear, 'an easy life'. This is only one kind of game that is played.

There are many others regarding power...

Such power games run rife through all organisations and it takes courage not to play them. That's why power is often defined by the courage that a person has to use their power to *not* collude with others and stand their own ground.

Executive Boards will sometimes discuss how they wish their staff to be "empowered". They may even make it an edict to their managers, that they "empower their staff" believing that by saying this, it will happen. Subtle power games occur whenever groups of people work together, especially when different levels of 'Wands of Authority' are handed out to different people; and it will never change under the directive of 'empowering everyone'. A better understanding of power and people is required.

In each situation, a person has the power of themselves, with the intelligence and range of individual freedoms and responsibilities of who they are. In work, their role and the wand of authority they have been granted act as a constraint on their personal power. Power in the workplace is not the expression of the power of a person in their entirety, but rather the power that relates to their job, and what it may or may not decide about. For example, a receptionist meets and greets people in the business, takes their name, signs them in and informs them about the health and safety features of the premises, and arranges for a person to meet them. Their role may not be given the power to manage other people around them. Such segmentation creates an awareness of the limitation of role and responsibility, and therefore of power.

This is why organisations who delegate full authority to a person dealing with customers get such fantastic results. They allow their people to think for themselves and to act in whatever ways to satisfy their customer; and because they are able to use the whole of themselves, their intelligence and their humanity to create solutions that are satisfying to customers, people feel empowered. The whole of the person is engaged in solving the problem and they are not restricted by bureaucracy.

Whilst attending an evening presentation on Corporate Risk, one of the presenters told a story of an industrial accident which had resulted in a major fire, destroying machinery and building and costing millions of pounds. When the investigators looked into the cause of the accident, they were able to trace the problem to a fitment around a pipe which had obviously been worn and not replaced in good time. When they looked further into it, they were able to trace several emails from the engineer to his manager, who had identified the problem, requesting that a new fitment be bought. (He did not have the power to order it himself because he had no mandate to spend money.) His manager had not authorised the purchase of that fitment because the policy of the company at the time was that anything above £150 had to be given permission by Head Office. The manager had requested permission but it had been overlooked. The fitment cost £200. Had either the engineer or the manager had the power to exercise their own power to buy what was needed, the accident would never have happened.

There is a paradox between power and responsibility which every organisation is trying to deal with, in relation to what power each person can be given and what responsibility they want to take. Some companies are extremely prescriptive on what each role is supposed to do and HR officers spend huge amounts of time and effort working out competency frameworks and role descriptions to define these for each person, level and function.

The descriptions of each role is metaphorically laid as a box upon a person and that person is then engaged in a struggle to either get out of the box, be promoted out of that box, change what they can do in the box but most often, they feel uncomfortable in the box. Most people's job description is an imposition that doesn't fit them. This is because every human being is an individual unlike any other, with talents, power and capabilities far greater than one role.

In the last two hundred years in Europe and the US, business has been about systemising the processes, functions and activities that go on in the business, which has meant considering every person as a part of that mechanism. This has led to de-powering people down to act as a function, rather than a person with intelligence and power to meet non-mechanistic situations. As an example — organisations like Amazon who use people to stack shelves, find books, pack them and other logistical functions — narrow down the person to the functionality of doing the work and limiting their power to do solely that job. This restriction and de-powering down of people has huge impacts into their health and well-being. Whereas freeing people to use their innate power means allowing them to be more widely functional and to use a wider range of themselves; ultimately benefitting the company as well.

Power Position

A person or small group who have great power can exercise their power to create a set of conditions that impacts many others (eg. an executive board can determine the initiation of a change programme that will cut staff numbers by 10 per cent). It is often very clear to employees that they have little power to change such decisions. Those engaged in implementing the decision may be able to determine who specifically will be fired and may have a little power to adjust how it gets done. HR personnel attempt to create processes that make it appear fairer, but the lack of power that employees have is starkly evident throughout such processes. This always leads to a feeling of disempowerment in all staff (including those not affected), because they recognise if it can happen to their colleagues, it can and may happen to them. This is called 'survivor syndrome' and has been a regular feature of many organisations in the last decade.

This holds true for the majority of organisations, but it need not be so. In organisations like the John Lewis Partnership, the power structures are very different. They have a democratic model that shares power amongst all staff. Each partner is recognised as an owner of the business and therefore their power can extend everywhere that they may personally choose to extend it, whilst taking the responsibilities that go with their idea/proposal/suggestion or action. Partners have a voice within all strategic decisions that may need to be taken within the organisation – in shutting a warehouse down, opening up a new store, cutting staff – and their challenge to any such ideas must be addressed by the leadership. Partners also have access to the Partnership Council (the highest level of spokespersons for the employees) which engages in vigorous debate on all issues raised by the Partners. Partners may even challenge the Chairman and his activities, demonstrating a very different view about power.

Power within the John Lewis Partnership is distributed to all staff, and the power of those at the top are moderated by a set of checks and balances which truly empowers all Partners and makes them accountable for the whole organisation, its present and future development. The power structure promotes communication through all levels and tiers of Partners. The power of each individual (the Partner) is recognised and has a place within the decision making function of the organisation. By structuring such restraints upon the power exercising authorities of the executive level, the organisation ensures that leaders understand that power is equally distributed and they don't have permission to act outside of what has been widely agreed. This breeds a certain kind of humility and respect, allowing leaders and managers to listen to each others' views and promotes understanding between them.

In legal or accounting Partnerships there is a distinct difference of power between the owners of the business – the equity partners – and everyone else. Most partnerships retain control of power in their hands, delegating much or little according to the enlightened approach or not, of the majority of partners.

Power in Hierarchies

In a hierarchical company, it is important for a new leader to recognise that immediately upon their promotion or elevation to leadership, there will be an automatic increase of power at their disposal. One of the ways that I explain it to some of my clients is through this metaphor: They won't have to have done anything – merely the announcement going out, whether verbal or email, will mean that all those who hear of it, will now see them differently. That difference is an extra unit of power that each person will now attribute to them. That unseen credit, that one unit of power that each person gives them will mean an increase of amperage of power available to them as leader.

It's no use to ignore this, or try to pretend that they haven't changed, or don't wish to or expect to change. It's like them thinking they are King Canute and expecting the ocean not to come in. It will and there isn't anything that they can do about it. In a hierarchical structure, Power changes people and situations, whether they or anyone else wishes it to. Pretending that nothing has changed and insisting on carrying on in the same way as before is to invite manifold problems.

Now there is an unspoken contract that is created by the person awarding the unit of power to the new leader which is never spoken or acknowledged, and leaders get into trouble when they don't hold up their end of the bargain (which of course they don't consciously know about). This is why empathy and intuition are very valuable qualities in leaders and why leaders whose capabilities are not so great in this area, use coaches such as myself, to explain this contract to them. For the contract is this: *"I will give you some of my units of power, if you then make my life better."*

The problem for new leaders is evident when colleagues now expect something different from them; in fact, they expect many different things that won't become clear to the person who's struggling to do what they've always done. Taking on a bigger role successfully means asking the following:

- How will you make your staff's life better because you are now their leader?
- How you are going to make a better environment or circumstance for those around you because you now have greater power?

- What power will you delegate and to whom?
- What must you now stop doing and delegate to your managers and colleagues?
- What will you pass on to help them, grow them, and improve their chance of promotion?
- What activities do you need to retain or take on, to help you fulfil your new leadership role?

Enlightened leaders operating in a hierarchical situation need a perspective that's bigger, broader and less directive, in terms of impact and results. A manager and director will look to get results and achievements in their areas of responsibility. A leader looks for impact into the larger organisation, whether it's a better behavioural model that they are promoting or a change initiative that will lead to new values being demonstrated such as diversity.

A leader with power creates impact. They are happy to make that impact because they're confident enough to believe that their views, perceptions, attitudes, style or contribution are of value beyond themselves. Self-esteem is necessary and a self-image that they are comfortable to demonstrate and make known to the wider context of the whole organisation.

This shouldn't mean that the leader throws their weight around and have a view about everything that doesn't relate to them. No. If their behaviour makes the organisation worse, because they want to exercise their power to now control more 'domain or territory' then conflicts and silo working will become features of the environment. If such leadership behaviours, born of exercising their newly awarded power, begin to deliver negative results, they should be demoted, because they cannot control the power that's been given to them.

Hierarchical structures create power structures and the way that a new leader will handle power can quickly be determined. Whether they consciously decide to use their power for constructive results, (that do not glorify themselves but benefit others working for them,) will demonstrate much about how they will lead over the longer term and what benefits they will bring to the people around them. Enlightened leaders can exercise power in such circumstances by having constructive conversations to elicit the concerns of the wider stakeholder groups.

In global corporations, the range of power is institutionalised and structured so that people are required to act in accordance with that power structure. Thinking or acting from themselves is not always encouraged. Recent innovations in the Compliance function (now sometimes extended to Ethics and Compliance) attempts to act as the check and balance to these power structures, by encouraging people to act in accordance with a Code of Conduct and to report infringements of ethical or company policies. A Help Line is often provided, encouraging individuals to discuss any possible infringements and gain support to report any bad practises. Whistle blowing at illegal or bad practices in a company is now growing, but protecting individuals who report such mal-practise is not often feasible.

The differential between the power of the individual and the corporation (which has at its command large sums of money as well as resources of lawyers, accountants and people with a wide spectrum of expertise that can be activated on its behalf) demonstrates the differential of power against the individual. This keeps in check any individual wanting to act on their own, to change things for the better or report illegal, unethical or company policy infringements. The price they may pay is often loss of their employment, as well as extra personal stresses and pressures that may lead to loss of well-being.

Abuses of Power

In *'23 Things They don't tell you about Capitalism'* by Ha-Joon Chang, a notable economist dissects the economic justifications that free-market economists have provided corporate and political leaders to place businesses above the rule of law and beyond the reach of just and fair contracts. In Chapter 13 'Making rich people richer doesn't make the rest of us richer' he highlights the deregulation that has taken place in the US and UK allowing companies to 'make bigger profits, not least because they were more able to exploit their monopoly powers, more freely pollute the environment and more readily sack workers.' The resulting income inequality and the concentration of greater and greater income into the executive level of businesses have meant concentration of power at that level. This power has been used to provide greater benefits, greater salaries and greater power in a concentrated section of the executive working class – the upward re-distribution of wealth, which has actually slowed down growth in the world's economies.

He advocates giving billions of dollars to lower income households because *"The economy-boosting effect of the extra billion dollars given to the lower-income households through increased welfare spending will be bigger than the same amount given to the rich through tax cuts."* Additionally, he recognises that *"greater income equality may promote social peace by reducing industrial strikes and crime, which may in turn encourage investment, as it reduces the danger of disruption to the production process and thus to the process of generating wealth."**

The power of the managerial class was most vividly demonstrated in the aftermath of the 2008 financial crisis, when the American and the British governments injected astronomical sums of taxpayers' money into troubled financial institutions in the autumn of 2008, *'few of the managers who were responsible for their institution's failure were punished... The fact that the British and the American taxpayers, who have become the shareholders of the bailed-out financial institutions, cannot even punish their now-employees for poor performance and force them to accept a more efficient compensation scheme shows the extent of power that the managerial class now possesses in these countries.* **

"Markets seek out inefficient practices, but only when no-one has sufficient power to manipulate them... one-sided managerial compensation packages impose huge costs on the rest of the economy while they last. The workers have to be constantly squeezed through downward pressure on wages, casualization of employment and permanent downsizing, so that the managers can generate enough extra profits to

distribute to the shareholders and keep them from raising issues with high executive pay." This abuse of power is now being recognised to be widespread, pervasive and all-encompassing at the corporate level.

The situation was originally created by an ethos that was supposedly going to lead to the distribution of wealth and wellbeing to all people. 'Trickle down economics' has however, failed to deliver on its promises to make the poor better off. According to Ja-Joon Chang, worker pay in the US has been virtually stagnant since the mid 1970's whilst CEO's pay has risen dramatically – instead of 30 - 40 times greater than the average worker compensation, it is now 300 - 400 times greater. As well as being paid excessive amounts these managers do not get punished for bad management, even when they lose their job they almost always get a huge severance payment cheque. * p154

It is an abuse of power to pay executives (and even footballers, celebrities and film stars) the huge amounts that they are paid for their work. What is a fair number of multiples for the differential between oil rig worker employed out on an oil rig in Indonesia or the CEO of a major FTSE company? Is it 5, 10, 20, or 100 or even 1000 times more? Or what is a fair multiple between a professional sitting in their London office and their CEO and that oil rig worker in Indonesia? What is a fair multiple of difference between your wages and your boss, or your MD? Does it feel fair? Is it based on some rationale, or is it the lame excuse of "It's a competitive market-place and we have to pay a competitive price to get the best?"

Executives in the corporate context exercise great power over such things as wages, promotion, recognition and bonuses of all employees. Leaders using that greater power can give more respect and benefits to their workers, or they can choose to abuse that power to give less and give themselves more. They can be fair, or they can be unfair, by exercising the choices available to them. *They have come to control the board-rooms through interlocking directorship and manipulation of information that they provide to independent directors, and as a result few boards of directors question the level and the structure of executive pay'.*

It is these irrational differentials that make people mad and want to overthrow their governments, or their corporate structures. Joseph E. Stiglitz in *'The Price of Inequality'* draws the comparison of the Arab Spring where ordinary citizens overthrew their corrupt governments with the suggestion that it may happen in the US, unless strong measures are undertaken to introduce a more balanced distribution of power; especially in the moderation of the power of corporations and the corporate giveaways and welfare awarded them by their government.

The flatter an organisation, the less opportunity there is for such power games to be played; hence many technology companies attempt to promote very different ways of working in teams without designated leaders, etc. Google, ARM, Redgate Software and many other technology companies have pioneered ways that devolve power to lower levels of staff, or they have little hierarchy. Some of these ways have been constructed into a new form of internal governance by Brian J. Robertson and described in his book *'Holocracy: The Revolutionary Management System that Abolishes Hierarchy'*.

Where power is institutionalised and structured so that people are allotted more or less power (with regard to their role and activity within the organisation) everyone is indoctrinated into believing their place in the structure is also their place in the power system that the organisation has set up. People can come to believe that their personal power is that which they experience at work. The film 'Made in Dagenham' is marvellous because it shows women not accepting a disempowered position that everyone around them assumes, from the senior managers, executives, fellow male workers and even their male partners. They choose instead to exercise their personal power to go on strike and to demand equal pay for equal work under the banner of justice.

In ancient times, when a Roman General returned from battle, popular belief says that as he was parading through the streets during a victory triumph, standing behind him was his slave, tasked with reminding the general that, although at his peak today, tomorrow he could be brought down. The servant advises *"Respice post te! Hominem te esse memento! Memento mori!"* meaning *"Look behind you! Remember that you are a man! Remember that you'll die!"* as noted by Tertullian in his *Apologeticus*. Many an employee would like to say these very same sentiments to one or other of their leaders!

This is what CEOs who think they are invincible because they have power and control should remember. The power they exercise is not theirs and only temporarily given them to use for a short time. Should they not use it well, their tenure may be vilified and criticised, with their mistakes, shortcomings and personal flaws made clear in articles and books. Will the many millions they draw from the business be fair recompense for the vilification they will receive?

Different Uses of Power

In the history of capitalism, some leaders behaved in ways in advance of their times to use their power to aid their workers in humane ways. Joseph Rowntree is one such example. He was always determined to produce top quality confectionary, and equally determined to ensure that fair wages were paid to his workers. He sought to create a high level of well-being and welfare for his workforce. He was aware of the social conditions in which many of his factory workers lived and he improved the quality of their life by providing affordable, decent housing, recreational facilities and even education. He had a unique approach to poverty, at a time when there was little understanding of what poverty even meant.

The Rowntree Company provided a source of income for thousands of families right around the world. It introduced professional standards in the business environment, long before such things were commonplace. Joseph Rowntree was an active philanthropist throughout his life, working to improve adult literacy, and safeguarding democracy and political fair play. He drew attention to the need to tackle the root causes of poverty, not just its immediate symptoms and the Rowntree Charitable Trust continues to apply their philanthropy to accomplish this. Today, it provides support to people who are addressing the root causes of conflict and injustice; as well as those who are challenging the existing power imbalances in society in order to effect real change. They take a long view to support change towards a better world.

Today we live in a time when questions have re-emerged about philanthropy and corporate social responsibility, as well as questions about how we can achieve a fair and compassionate society.

Authority and Power

In his book *'The Righteous Mind'* Jonathan Haidt says there is an *"Authority Condition. Look in two directions up toward superiors and down toward subordinates. These modules work together to help individuals meet the adoptive challenges of forging beneficial relationships within hierarchies. We are the descendants of the individuals who were best able to play the game — to rise in status while cultivating the protection of superiors and the challenge of subordinates."* He says *"It makes us sensitive to signs of rank or status and to signs that other people are (or are not) behaving properly, given their position"*.

The important point he makes is that groups of people have a sensitivity and awareness about how others may be using their authority to benefit themselves and when they benefit those around them.

If people in power do not behave properly – ie., they grant themselves excessive benefits and pay — then those around them will act to correct the imbalance. The indignation and horror that most people have about banks and their power that has brought governments to their knees, has not yet been fully expressed. It will be, and watch out world as subtle changes come into being with people changing their behaviour to cut their reliance and use of banks.

Based on my research and discussion with many people, this will lead to very fundamental changes in the financial services industries. Banks will shrink – not just in the numbers of people who are employed by them — but their capital structure will shrink as their ability to create money from nothing will be nullified by people and organisations no longer willing to buy into their creations (whether they are interest rate swaps, currency swaps, mortgage obligations, debt obligations etc.).

"Group selection pulls for co-operation, for the ability to suppress anti-social behaviour and spur individuals to act in ways that benefit their groups." Jonathan Haidt suggests co-operation is the required standard of behaviour for social groupings that act in concert; wider co-operation for social and welfare improvement is required for the inequalities of small groups benefitting themselves are to be changed to benefit the majority.

Whilst I was presenting to a group of University staff and students, they asked to discuss power. In the ensuing conversation they declared that their bosses took power for themselves, whilst disempowering and ignoring them; yet, another issue appeared to be their own internal fears to confront or change this situation. Their own anxieties and concerns caused them to restrict exploring how they might respond differently to correct the situation. They took no responsibility for accepting or making things different. They all agreed that that their bosses were abusing their position to benefit themselves, whilst diminishing the rights and freedoms of their staff. But their acceptance of this was also part of the problem. This suggests a common culture, with common stories can blind individuals to the power available them.

Power is available to all humans – it's part of their human allowance — and choice to exercise it is part of that allowance. Leaders have power over many more things and they can exercise that greater power to give more respect to their workers, or they can choose to abuse that power and give less, by giving themselves more. They can be fair, or they can be unfair, by exercise of the choices and opportunities available to them.

ENLIGHTENED LEADERS PERSPECTIVE

Leaders with self-awareness recognise that they always have a choice about how to use the power they have – and in business contexts, power is mostly used to determine other people's activities and the organisation's strategic objectives. So power is traditionally concerned with external factors.

Enlightened leaders look at power from a different standpoint. They recognise that in having power they need to use it to make changes in the thing they most have power over – themselves. They think, like Mahatma Gandhi, that you need to *"Be the change that you wish to see in the world."* And that *"As human beings, our greatness lies not so much in being able to remake the world – that is the myth of the atomic age – as in being able to remake ourselves."* The personal development journey is always an internal one; before a person can influence or impact another in a positive way.

The human principles I have outlined in this book are not so hard if as a private person you go about your life not wanting to exercise your personal power to make much of an impact in the wider world, but sincerely living with truth, respect, fairness and integrity. Life challenges us all however, and even with that scope, each of us is confronted with how much truth we will live by, how much respect we will extend to those we interact with and how much selfishness or fairness we will use to define our relationships.

By acknowledging the personal power available to you, you can become far more self-determining about how you think and how you feel and what actions you will choose to take. The world around you will change when you do so. Not only because you are now viewing your environment through new lenses of thoughts and emotions but also because the change within can allow you to take action in ways you wouldn't have – or maybe even have thought about – while stuck in your old thought patterns.

If you change yourself, you will change your world. The examples I have highlighted in this book – Joseph Rowntree, George Cadbury, John Spedan Lewis and Ove Arup — had the courage to go against the accepted business norms of their time and used their power to be different from others around them. Undoubtedly they would have reflected on the internal principles that drove them, to get clear on what they stood for, what was important as against unimportant, and had to practise in themselves the very things that they held important, before they could then confront the differences between themselves and others in their relationships.

Every business leader mentioned above will have had partners or co-directors who they had to convince to give up the privileges of ownership or financial rewards and to divert monies or put their shares in trust for the benefit of employees. This cannot have been easy and only personal conviction and alignment to human principles will have helped them impact and persuade others of the validity for taking such radical measures, compared to the norms of the day.

Enlightened leaders recognise the difficulty of effecting change in others (because they have experienced how difficult it is to change themselves), so become aware that how they role model and provide examples to others are the most powerful ways to demonstrate the changes they would like others to make. Personal power emanates from the core of a person to others outside them – those closest to them first, then to second and third degrees of separation – so that influencing others becomes a natural outcome of powerfully held beliefs and practices.

The picture below demonstrates in diagrammatic form how enlightened leaders exercise power. They apply power and energy towards themselves first, to clarify how they apply the principles of truth, respect, justice and fairness in their own lives to build an integrity that they can consciously be aware of and from which they can make decisions. They use that power to decide what they will and will not do, and to decide what issues are important and what to prioritise from them. Only after these are clear, should power be used to influence others, in personal relationships and the work environment and organisation. For leaders directing organisations which impact in a major way the community and environment, the clarity of the inner work accomplished around principles will bear fruit to benefit, rather than harm the wider community.

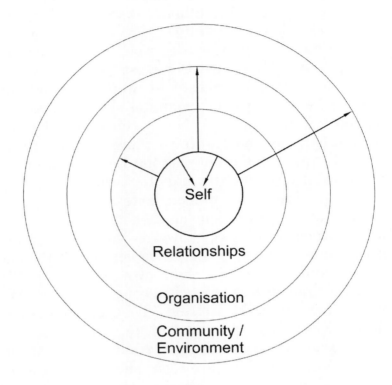

Figure 3: How enlightened leaders exercise power

Personal power aligned with natural human principles can and does have impact and influence upon people far beyond just a rational argument. So moving from impacting other people in relationship to you, enlightened leaders can make changes in their organisation, which can then in turn, make substantive differences in the community and environment in which the organisation operates. (The powers of the human principles that John Spedan Lewis and Ove Arup expressed are reflected in the practices and activities by which their organisations operate today.)

Enlightened leaders recognise that the organisational culture that they work in is largely the creation of their thinking and their practices, along with the cohort of leaders beside them. They take their personal responsibility seriously and exercise their power with conscious awareness. Through their mindsets, their attitudes and behaviours, they influence others to see the world the way that they see it and to respond in similar ways. Over time, this continuous role-modelling influences others to adopt similar mindsets, similar behaviours and attitudes. In this way, groups of people then think and act in similar ways, creating cultures that embody the principles of truth, respect, fairness and justice and that operate with integrity and trustworthiness.

It is through the formation of such constructive relationships and cultures that our collective consciousness and humanity grows.

Chapter Eleven

GETTING BACK ON THE HUMANE TRACK

EMBEDDING THE HUMANITY PRINCIPLES

"The market will demand over time the emergence of principled companies. These companies will not be long on rhetoric alone. They won't just have fancy PR and advertising slogans. They won't necessarily even wear their morality on their sleeve. What they will do is bake principle and purpose into the very DNA of the firm and how they operate."

Ira Jackson, Former Director, Centre for Business & Government, Kennedy School at Harvard, in the documentary film 'The Corporation'

It is one thing for us to consider the Humanity principles and like philosophers discuss their value and how they might play out in practice, rectifying the problems we see around us in our minds. It is quite another to consider embedding them into our working practices. The psychological patterns of our capitalist system have been created over hundreds of years and changing them will not be easy.

Where we are now, shows us the ultimate, unpleasant end place that the market economy, (built upon competition and a sole focus on profit) will lead us to. Altogether, these results may be serious enough as to alert us all to the need for change.

The question has to be "How do we do that"?

To some degree, the answers are innate in all of us – we have merely forgotten. We need a reminder of what humanity looks like, feels like and acts like; we need to make conscious again the important benefits we derive when we act from humane principles. We need to remember that if we leave the power of corporations unchecked, a few individuals can severely damage our health, wellbeing and financial wellbeing. So more of us, who I call Enlightened Leaders, need to exercise our power of choice and bring our intelligence into play to make our working environments humane.

Getting Started — Assembling a Compelling Case — Primary Reasons Why We Must Change

The current business code has been operative for over four hundred years. If we are to change it, we need strong compelling reasons. We need to begin by challenging a range of assumptions that are inherent in the current system and then identify alternative ways to engage in realignment to the humane track.

There are eight very good reasons why we need to embed the Humanity principles into our thinking and the working practises of our organisations today which will affect the future of our world. Some of these arguments represent a 'burning platform' that requires all of us to change, whilst others are the herald of change already happening. We may notice these change occurring in small but pertinent ways, pointing out the wave that is already upon us and which we need to get ahead of, as the curve of change appears in the new generation of people populating our world.

Eight Reasons

1. Stop damaging people
2. Clean up unhealthy toxic workplace environments
3. Create fairness in the supply chain
4. Make contracts fair
5. Engage employees in right thinking
6. Follow the signs for future ways of thinking
7. Evolve human consciousness towards purposeful and meaningful work
8. Create new economic models

1. Stop damaging people

Biologists have physical examples to show us that where a species is subject to toxicity in its environment, it will cause it to decline, or even die. Tigers, elephants, whole varieties of fish, now even bees are being wiped out as the environment in which the specie thrived becomes toxic, or unsustainable. I have witnessed extensive damage to individual people, identifiable as 'burnout', mental ill-health, stress, anxieties, and even suicide. Japan's *karoshi* deaths are the tip of an iceberg of death occurring because of over-work. Western companies hide the damage they do through non-disclosure agreements and financial payments.

Physical toxicity kills, but so does internal toxicity – of feelings, of the ethical and moral kind.

We need to acknowledge our humanity and to recognise that we need more truthful, respectful, humane and fair relationships to make people's working lives healthier. Reconnecting to and embedding an ethical framework like the Humanity Principles will turn us away from a disaster trajectory back towards an alignment that is natural against our human feelings and design.

2. Clean up unhealthy toxic environments

More global disasters of the environmental and financial kind that we have experienced in recent years will occur if organisations continue along the path of no Integrity, little Respect, little Truth, Unfairness and Injustice. They will make our work contexts unhealthy by breeding corporate selfishness, abuse, illegal collusions, inequality and racism. Organisations that have the power to pollute our planet even more than at present can harm people as well as cause damages in climate change that may be irreparable. (Volkswagen's engineers practised deceit in order that their cars appeared to meet emission levels, which meant more cars were sold, but polluted the environment whilst driven.)

This will lead to the point where employees will not want to work for such organisations, suppliers will not want to supply them and customers will boycott them. The human race has a powerful history of correcting institutions that have gone wrong and there are manifold examples of businesses that pay a huge price for their unethical behaviours (Enron, Arthur Andersen and Royal Bank of Scotland all come to mind).

3. Create fairness in the supply chain

Organisations who thrive on an unequal wielding of power or un-transparent or unfair practices, will be identified and hurt through media coverage keen to name and shame bad behaviour. If an organisation lays its emphasis upon delivering the best value to its customers, it can, as Tesco did, squeeze its suppliers in such a way that they could not profit by any transaction with them. This actually led to complaints from customers, who boycotted them.

If, as an organisation you have permitted your systems to exploit any group or individuals who have directly or indirectly supplied their goods or services to you, you need to correct these injustices and act to re-balance those relationships. If you don't, such imbalanced relationships will hurt your reputation, damage your brand trust, lose customers and lay your organisation open to legal damages.

The opposite of this is to create opportunities to add value in the world not just through what you do, but through your supply chain. The Body Shop is a good case in point. They recognise and value their suppliers, seeking out the good that they can deliver to them, by including farmers and growers of the basic commodities that go into their products. Waitrose and John Lewis build trust throughout their supply chain, by respecting and being fair to the suppliers who produce the products they sell. They are committed "to a better way of doing business and being fair in all our business relationships."

4. Make contracts fair

Organisations that have contracts that benefit themselves whilst taking advantage of their employees, customers or suppliers will be building in resentments into their relationships and damaging trust. This will cost them one way or another. Employees who feel taken advantage of are much more likely to steal or short-change their employer with sick days and time off.

Leaders should review contracts to make them fairer in terms of quality, timings and profit margins. Improve relationships by admitting to errors and agree improved new standards. These may cost you up front, but over time the improved perception of the people who you deal with will lead to improved performance and better relationships that can lead to improved win-win opportunities. When two parties in a contract believe that fairness is at play, creative and innovative possibilities that cannot be conceived of when two parties are in antagonism and protection.

5. Engage employees in right thinking

Creating a healthy ecology and environment where Integrity, Respect, Truth, Trust and Justice thrive, means creating a clean environment that is based on firm rules and clear accountabilities where staff are aware of penalties for bad behaviour, as well as rewards for good. Clean environments support the health and well-being of your staff, your customers and your suppliers. If you don't, as many banks have continued to find out, you will be subject to lawsuits, fines and penalties from regulators as your staff continue to practise wrong doing, (rig markets, practice collusion and insider trading).

Different industries have their own demons to re-train (eg., the General Motors 'ignition switch scandal' where GM employees allegedly knew about vehicle faulty ignition switches blamed for at least 13 deaths and 54 serious accidents. GM was forced to release internal documents disclosing this knowledge and to finally initiate a vehicle recall in February 2011). This will support the health and well-being of your staff and the customers whom they serve. This can be done by ironing out inequalities of rewards, dealing with everyone with respect, instituting systems that allow everyone to grow, develop and progress. It will cut down your problems and enable you and your Executive team to focus on how to best lead, through your creativity, your innovation and your good intentions.

6. Follow the signs for future ways of thinking

There may be other compelling arguments and other compelling evidence that signals change (some of which will happen whether we wish for it to or not). According to current research, Generation Y workers make up roughly 25% of the world population – that's 1.75 billion people. The accelerating increase in population numbers world-wide in the past 50 years has led to an enormous increase in the amount of people who fall into the category of Generation Y, so it is one of the largest generational categories. In contrast, the world population is approximately 21% Generation X, and 18% Baby Boomers.

The Gen Y population thinks and acts quite differently from Gen X or Baby Boomers. Roughly 21% of the American workforce was Generation Y as of 2009, showing a rapid increase since 2005, when it was 14%. Approximately % of the adult population of the UK is Generation Y and a similar percentage of Generation Y adults make up the population of Canada. Within India, roughly half of the population is under the age of 25, (approximately 600 million) an astonishingly large number of people being trained in the Generation Y way of mind at the moment. The Generation Y population of China consists of approximately 200 million people.

Gen Y's psychographics are very different. Far from the 'work hard, get rich' attitude of earlier generations the Generation Y workers adopt a more relaxed demeanour, geared more towards the fulfilment of personal goals, having more autonomy in what they do and being one's own boss. Today's children live in a world where diversity prevails. Not only is society increasingly multicultural, but kids today are used to a range of global viewpoints, an array of non-traditional family types and different sexual alignments from an early age. Gen Y attitudes reflect an interest in and acceptance of diversity in many areas of life. They think it's OK to be disruptive and to challenge what's being said or done. They have a mentality that will challenge the status quo, and already challenges the profit motive as the primary *raison d'être* of business.

7. Evolve human consciousness towards purposeful and meaningful work

Our world-wide human consciousness (suggested by the idea of the collective unconscious as described by Carl Jung) is evolving towards identifying and living a purposeful life that serves our wider human needs, rather than only gaining financial rewards, buying and owning lots of stuff and being able to put food on the table. (Though there are still billions of people for whom surviving and putting food on the table is still a daily pervasive purpose.) For those of us who have the ability to recognise this consciousness, it calls us to make our work be of service to others (and perhaps this work can be of help to the billions who don't have the luxury) that we may do 'good' in the world.

If your organisation doesn't promote a worthwhile purpose, many people will not work for you. This new consciousness is appearing in concentrate amongst the GenY generation who have as a primary concern, the principles of an organisation, when deciding whether they would work for them. If organisations wish to appeal to such a workforce, they need to identify the good they seek to do in this world and explain it well.

8. Create new economic models

Somewhere in the near future, economists will start asking how we can have a market economy that is not based upon ever-increasing consumption levels. Considerations such as:-

How can we have a capitalist system NOT based upon ever increasing growth and profit levels?

How can we create a society based upon organisations delivering value, being paid for that value, but not necessarily delivering ever increasing dividends to its shareholders?

How can we create a global economy that doesn't rely on continuing increases in population for growth and success?

How can economies function efficiently without the international discrepancies of wealth and poverty?

How can we have successful businesses that are not reliant upon the exploitation of the weakest and the poorest by the richest?

Stock Exchange Listings and Corporate Governance — do these promote or take away from organisations considering their impact upon human beings? It often appears that these are tick the box exercises to demonstrate compliance at an informational level, rather than accountable activities that the organisation ties themselves and their employees to making effective; to create the impression of compliance with the law, rather than living inside the context of the law. For example, Integrated Reporting is an attempt to recognise the multiple responsibilities and impacts of organisations and the executives who run them. Do they serve the people employed by them, the countries in which they operate, the social environment, the physical environment?

Our world-wide economies are no longer responding in the traditional text book ways that originated in Adam Smith's 'Causes of the Wealth of Nations' (1776). Countries such as Switzerland are demonstrating that deflation can still allow growth in a country without the damaging side-effects. Government interference in the form of quantitative easing is not leading to the economic revivals of growth and inflation that they anticipate. These are all signs pointing to the need for new thinking in the economic sphere. Traditional economic models as practised by global corporations have lead to so much that is damaging that even Nobel Prize Winner Joseph E. Stiglitz and other living economists today are highlighting their problems and showing how a fairer system of economics can be introduced. Michael J. Sandel asserts that there should be a moral limit to markets. I suggest that there should be morality inside markets and business.

We need to re-draw boundaries so that economics has less territory and so that humanity can have more, in our psychologies, our mental constructs and our work-place focus.

Getting Started – With Leaders

Leaders have a powerful opportunity to create a wish list for the things they would like to see in the world, as well as in their workplace. What contribution would they like their organisation to make in the global environment? What would an ideal workplace look like, in terms of the qualities at play?

A company's leaders must provide a vision for the organisation that has a higher purpose than just money, profits or becoming number one in a market. Their imagination and creativity is called for to build opportunities that are going to make our world a better place. This is vital not just for personal connection and satisfaction of its employees, but for its long term financial performance. This is demonstrated many times in Jim Collin's *'Good to Great'*. Leaders need to recognise that 'For a wise man to think it, is to create it' and each employee has a part to play in that creation.

"Enlightened leaders and business managers throughout the world have used this simple principle in one way or another for many years. They know that when people are meaningfully involved, they willingly commit the best that is in them. Moreover, when people identify their personal goals with the goals of an organisation, they release an enormous amount of energy, creativity, and loyalty." Stephen R. Covey – *Principle Centred Leadership.*

As this book is intended for Enlightened Leaders I need to ask the question 'What are the personal changes that leaders will need to make in themselves before they can implement an enlightened and humanity principled way forward for others?' Organisations can't change without leaders changing first. What are the personal changes that leaders might need to make in their own psyche and attitudes? It is by asking and pursuing meaningful answers to the following questions that enlightened leaders are created.

The challenges that face them are to determine where they are and how far their personal psychologies are embedded in the market economy? Whether they can even assess accurately the value of the Humanity Principles inside business? Can they understand the value that thinking differently would bring them and their organisation? What is the balance of their focus between customer, employees, shareholders, and Executive Board? How do these different stakeholders inter-relate and how sound and principled are the relationships between them? Are those relationships characterised by trust, respect, truth and justice? Where are the balances of power and how is power distributed amongst the organisational system?

Who do they currently think they serve? How much of their mind-sets are self-serving and what would it take to think in ways that enable them to be honest, respectful and have integrity? How big are the personal and collective blind-spots that restrict their seeing? Is it a matter of thinking of themselves in service to the organisation, to their staff, to their customers? Several books have been written about the 'Servant Leader' role if people want to look there. The capitalist system and market economy seems to have fixed the concept of the Board being in service to its shareholders and delivering value to them, which is why it is so liberating when there are no shareholders external to the employees to serve.

Leaders need to revisit the notion of delivering shareholder value and create a wider brief for themselves; especially when mostly only one third of profits go to shareholders, and the remaining two thirds go either to investment in the business or to pay bonuses to themselves and staff. Many organisations are patently not delivering on that ethos anyway, otherwise their shareholders would not be voting against their remuneration plans.

When this subject matter has been discussed, some executives suggest that it is only necessary to ask leaders and managers to behave in a principled way. They argue that they have defined and promoted strong values in their organisation and that this is sufficient to ensure that their leaders behave in ways that support their values. *"Principles are not values. The German Nazis, like the street gang members, shared values, but these violated basic principles."* Stephen R. Covey – *Principle Centred Leadership.*

The "behaviour" argument which has been so popular in training programmes for leaders and managers, is asking too little of them. Do we think so little of people that we ask them to "behave in a fair way", or do we ask them to be "be fair"? An act that does not carry the "being" is just an act, like an actor on a stage, and most employees see through acts. Even a good method actor, well-practiced in acting the feelings, emotions and behaviours of a person, cannot be wholly what they are trying to be. People know and sense the gap between an act and the reality.

It is important for leaders to be unbiased, neutral, to have a state of being in them that is conducive to human relations. This means having a state of Non-judgement, to be open to see an issue from many sides, to remain open and undecided, to consider different views, to be balanced and stay in an uncommitted viewpoint, to try to gain an elevated perspective in order to see all sides of the issue. It is hard for executives to gain this neutral unbiased perspective if they are defensive of their own privileges and benefits.

What transparency can be created to open up dialogues around justice and fairness of the organisation's culture? How do your employees feel as a result of the salary scales and differential levels that operate in their organisation? How honest can you be and how honest do you ask your staff to be with you, before you start squirming? How openly can employees ask questions relating to decisions being taken regarding new policies, recruitment or layoffs? If Directors are seen not to meet their fiduciary responsibilities, for example, can a HR business partner challenge the Director and hold them to account to a higher authority? The power systems of most organisations do not permit such accountabilities.

If there are rules for one class of people and another rule for others, inequality, injustice, unfairness, disrespect and distrust will thrive rather than Humanity. Who should stop this and why don't they? If it's an issue of power, or speaking truth to power, that makes them not able to, there is a serious dysfunction in the organisation and shareholders should beware. Fire the CEO before he takes them into very hot water that may lose them all of their financial investment.

Getting Started –
With The Executive Team and Board

If we are to change an organisation's focus, we need to change the people who exercise power within them. Research that suggests that for changes to occur in the value system and accompanying behaviours of an organisation, much relies on the top management team and their level of personal development. Due to the power systems discussed in the previous chapter, the leadership team is the strongest influencer of change; hence their willingness to examine, determine and agree on the principles and rules upon which they will run the business is the primary arbiter of stasis or change. It requires leaders to accept these rules and make themselves subject to them, rather than require absolute control and make themselves exempt from them.

The Executive team often operates at the lowest common denominator that its CEO will allow. If he allows the Executive team to engage in shouting matches, boyish, male oriented power plays and behave in chauvinistic ways, women will not want to participate. If anyone reading this can't believe that this could happen at a major corporate, to my knowledge this precise scenario has happened at several FTSE 100 companies within the last five years. (As it happens in the UK Parliament, it is certainly tolerated in the Executive team and Boardroom!)

Frankly a CEO whose egotism has grown so great that they've become self-aggrandising, with prejudices and unclear principles, judgements based on personal bias and who brooks no contradiction from their executive team, is not likely to question whether a more enlightened approach would benefit them and their company. Then not only is the CEO lost, but often the organisation also.

A change or adoption of humane principles in business needs to start at the top. The Chairman of the Board and the Main Board can often be unaware of the behavioural impacts of their choice of Executive teams. Even when they are aware, they are not able to materially change the Executive team's behaviours – they can only change the members. Choices for CEO's or CFO's are mostly made upon those executives' ability to execute, deliver and make profits. Personal values, character and personal principles are low in the priority list of sought-after characteristics.

Embedding the Humanity Principles is not for the faint-hearted. It is for leaders who can perceive the value that it can bring to pioneer a higher standard of life and the benefits it can bring to the people who work for them, for the customers who will benefit by them and the suppliers who will share their success.

It may begin with leaders for whom the Humanity Principles are personally very close to how they see the world and how they personally behave. Leaders with Integrity, Respect, Trust, Justice and Truth concerned for the legacy that their life and contribution can make to the world, whether it's a small business serving a local community or a global corporate interfacing with people in many countries through its services and products.

Embedding the Humanity Principles will not be attractive to business leaders who are just concerned for the next quarter's figures or the year-end bottom line – it's for visionaries who perceive how, by the choices they make today they will either improve our world, or detrimentally damage it. It's for leaders who genuinely want their business to NOT destroy the environment, who will NOT trade carbon credits in order to pollute our world more by their products' production processes, but are prepared to search out how to limit their business's negative impact upon our planet and its resources.

I recognise that anyone brave enough to want to incorporate a more enlightened ethos into their company is going to confront these challenges and will need to go into the process with their eyes wide open.

If we are to engender more humanity within the context of work, we need to address the specifics of how do we do that? We can be more humane, showing them what humanity looks like, feels like in relation to our co-workers, our customers and our suppliers. Read Tony Hsieh's book "Delivering Happiness" and make that required reading of all your leaders. Look for pointers on what you can change in your business to make positive contributions to the change that you and your employees would like to see happen. Bring the whole of yourself to work and permit employees to bring all of them to work with what that might mean. Invite them to identify and correct the challenges and issues of your business, rather than restricting them to doing a few things well.

A Cautionary Tale –
Challenges to Receiving Honest Feedback

It is likely that as an organisation, though not as an executive team, you have already been receiving significant feedback that you could be choosing to ignore. It may be your HR department knows a great deal that it is either choosing not to pass on, or they are passing on in small (to check your receptiveness) and because it's rejected, they do not pass on the full picture.

In my experience, as I have worked with organisations "attempting to change their culture", there are strong embedded reasons why the Executive team are not willing to hear, nor understand the feedback. In financial organisations for example, where a bonus culture is the norm, it doesn't matter how much newspapers castigate finance workers and CEO's about bonuses awarded, or the level of bonuses, they choose not to hear; nor do they wish to understand that it is not acceptable to pay bonuses when the organisation has become bankrupt and is only surviving due to money given it by a government or shareholders who expect their money to be put to good use and not to pay bonuses until the organisation is healthy and self-maintaining.

As individuals, if we fail to manage our finances poorly and get into significant debt, we have to undertake stringent measures to pay back what we owe and stop spending. Why should employees of that organisation not be subject to the same moral ethic? Is it because it's not their money they have lost, but ours?

In cases where the Executive team and senior staff benefit from a culture of personal benefits and bonuses, the most obvious truths do not sink in or penetrate because they want to hold onto the old paradigm, because only in the old paradigm do they get to keep the high salaries and benefits of working in businesses whose activities are so little understood. At a deeper level for all human beings, it is also about not wanting to admit to having done wrong before, which is why admitting to changing to a new paradigm is very hard.

An Organisational Audit will reveal any injustices or inequalities relating to gender, race, and salary differentials, overworking and under-paying staff, especially in industries where prejudices of various kinds reign. The challenge is whether the Executive Team will admit to them, and whether they will they have a willingness to change them?

What I have observed when the consideration of changes is raised, is that some individuals in power adopt the attitude of "Change is what others should do, *not* what I should do." Changing oneself is hard, even when you see the need and you understand the benefits the change will give you – eg., stopping smoking, leading a healthy exercise regime. When change means you will lose financial benefits, lose privileges, lose high status and even authority, change is unwelcome and hard to prosecute at a personal or group level.

The collective intelligence of people is accessible and available in all businesses, if only the Executive Team would accept a modicum of humility and were to ask for their input; and then honestly hear their answers. Your people and your organisations will tell you, unequivocally what the truth is where your organisation is concerned, just as long as you ensure a confidential process and ensure that you ask for genuine, authentic feedback.

Getting Started –
Creating Respect, Ownership and
Empowerment

The more organisations restrict their people's focus, responsibilities, attention and power, the less people will contribute. The more organisations open up people's opportunities to take ownership, be involved, be empowered, the greater the intelligence, energy and commitment will come forth from their people. This has been known for some time now, but I do not believe the price paid for not truly empowering and involving their employees has been calculated. The wider the brief employees are given, the greater the opportunities they have to bring their intelligence and humanity to bear upon all upon the issues, problems and challenge that exist within their context and environment.

These needs are being addressed in new models of organisation; Holocracy is a system of organisational governance devised by Brian J. Robertson in which authority and decision-making are distributed throughout a holarchy of self-organising teams rather than being vested in a management hierarchy. This has been adopted in for-profit and non-profit organisations in the US, France, Germany, Switzerland, New Zealand, Australia and the UK. Some high profile examples of companies who have used the Holocracy system are Zappos and Google. Such systems devolve power and responsibility to people who can effect needed changes promptly and accurately. Leaders can review how much of such a system can be introduced into their organisation.

By restricting people's responsibilities into narrowly defined roles and duties the more you narrow their opportunities to learn, grow and take responsibility. This may be useful for some juniors at the start of their career and development, but to maintain it as people grow and mature is to cut off their creativity, their stimulation and their enjoyment.

It may be that these concerns are already haunting senior leaders who have cut back their work-forces several times over in the last seven years. It may already be appearing in the minds of leaders running retail businesses that see how the internet will take away sales and will then call for lessening staff in their retail stores. It is certainly occupying the minds of many employees and managers. Therefore, the co-incidence of all these factors invites us to look for unusual solutions that cannot be found when looking along the economics line.

In some respect people may find these ideas and concepts very easy to assimilate and understand, especially in the context of their own private lives. These principles are not far off, or distant from how many people already live and experience the world. Being truthful, honest, fair, just is not hard for most people, most of the time. It's just that in the work context, the environment and its pressures and the cultural norms of the work-place can actually be more powerful.

Perhaps the most important thing to recognise is that an organisation is not a human being. It lacks the emotional experiences that humans have and therefore lacks the common language that humans share and trade with when communicating. This was most powerfully documented by Professor Joel Bakan in his book The Corporation, and the documentary film of the same name which was directed by Jennifer Abbott and Mark Achbar in 2003. The normal behaviours of psychopaths were explained in detail and then matched to examples of how many trans-national corporations have behaved in psychopathic ways, resulting in extreme inhumane outcomes. Professor Clive Boddy (Professor of Leadership and Organisation Behaviour at Middlesex University Business School in London) is also conducting research into corporate psychopathy and has found why some highly successful people with the condition might make it to Executive Board level.

All organisations are populated by people and they do have the capacity to think and feel. They can consider the Humanity Principles and how they might be applied. Here are some ideas for getting started:

Suggestions for Action

So what can be done by leaders seriously wishing to address this in the work context? They can do the following:

1. Clarify with colleagues in leadership what purpose their business exists to fulfil. Put this in writing and ask for input from all your employees. How do they see this issue and ask them to clarify their part in making the purpose happen?

2. What is the vision that you, the leadership and your employees can agree to, that enables them to see a bigger reason for why they do

what they do? What benefits do you deliver to your clients? Even mundane builders merchants can identify a vision that inspires - 'build a better world'?

3. Determine what ethical or moral principles you and they will use to make on the journey to the achievement of its purpose; ensuring that you're clear how Integrity, Respect, Truth, Trust, and Justice are to be applied in your business.

4. Put this in writing and open it up for challenge, comment and addition by your employees, some trusted external advisers and key personnel in trusted suppliers.

5. Agree who is to benefit and in what ways, by the existence and work of your organisation. Then organise your activities, processes and communications to make this happen.

6. Clarify what your duties are to be, in respect of the organisation's current aims and activities that will progress the organisation towards the fulfilment of its purpose.

7. State clearly what power is to be used and distributed amongst the various tiers of your organisation and how people are to be held accountable?

8. Define the principles that will operate inside the organisation to bring benefits to its employees and the environment.

9. Create rules and application standards that will ensure that this occurs and make specific people responsible to make it happen.

10. Define the principles that will apply to how the organisation will treat your suppliers and what checks and balances you will put in place in your processes and systems to ensure that your suppliers' workers are not being abused or exploited and if necessary check that they are appropriately recompensed and taken care of.

11. Define the principles that you will apply to the relationships that your employees will have with their local community and the part that you (and your employees) will play in contributing to its well-being and enhancement.

12. Engage all staff in these considerations and you will guarantee yourself a fair, just and highly intelligent outcome.

For reference with samples of how other organisations have practised such Human Principles, and the activities, processes and systems they've introduced to validate this process, refer to the next Chapter – *The Humane Track – What Success Looks Like.*

If your business is not at the stage that you can engage with your employees in the ways described above, and want to retrace a step, you can organise an Organisational Audit – not just to assess engagement, but to gain something a great deal more thorough about the organisation itself – the Truth of how it is experienced and felt by those who work in it. You can gain insights into how the leadership is valued and respected or not; and depending on who you ask, you can invite a great deal more information and a great deal more feedback from your suppliers (throughout the supply chain) and your customers. You can ask questions that relate to Integrity, Respect, Truth, Justice, Fairness and Trust, drawing from earlier questionnaires in the book, as well as those following here.

Organisational Audit Questionnaire

Suggested questions to include;

1. Do you feel that you are consistently dealt with in a humane manner by your company?

2. Do you feel that you are consistently dealt with in a humane manner by your manager?

3. Do you think that your company has humane principles at heart in the way it treats its employees?

4. Do you think that your company deals with its customers in a humane way?

5. Do you think the processes and systems of your organisation allow you to deal with your customers in a humane way?

6. Do you believe that your company deals with its suppliers in a humane manner?

7. Do you think you have the power to deal with your suppliers in a humane way?

8. What systems or processes do you think should be changed?

9. Do you think that your leaders speak the Truth about your company?

10. Are you invited to speak the truth to your leaders?

11. Do you respect your leaders?

12. Do your leaders respect their employees?

13. Do you think your leaders have integrity?

14. Is there congruency between your written contract and how you have to work?

15. Do you trust your leaders?

16. Do your leaders trust their employees?

17. Do you trust your manager?

18. Does your manager trust you?

19. If you could change anything in your company to make it a more humane place to work, in what areas would the changes be?

Truth	Respect	Fairness
Integrity	Trust	Power

20. Do you believe your leaders exercise power to make their lives better at the cost of their employees?

21. Do you believe that your leaders exercise power to benefit the company or to benefit themselves?

22. Do you feel empowered?

23. What power would you want to have that you currently do not have?

24. What are the three most important things you think need to be changed in your organisation?

Chapter Twelve

THE HUMANE TRACK

SAMPLES OF WHAT SUCCESS LOOKS LIKE

The central thesis of this work is that our reality as a human race, our 'Humanity' — issues from Principles that generate laws and rules that are common across all cultures and across all peoples. I have suggested that these principles are an inevitable consequence of natural ways that operate in human beings (with no difference deriving from cultural background) and that together, they can be constructed into a system. The Principles of this system (Truth, Respect, Justice, Integrity and Trust) can be understood to reflect the system's designed purpose and to work together to create an evolving consciousness through better alignment of thinking and behaviour; the effective operation or use of which, would be impossible if any one of the principles was to be ignored.

These fundamental Principles operate at a personal level in most people but have been assumed as present in the corporate arena when they have not been. Competition, capitalism and the free markets over several centuries have led to a situation where Truth, Respect, Justice, Integrity and Trust have been ignored and financial factors have become priorities of focus and the sole measure of success. The ignoring of these principles has undoubtedly led to many unhealthy patterns of behaviour at the individual and organisational level. What business has accomplished has interfered with the properly operating system of Humanity and has therefore translated into inhumane results – where we have seen exploitation, power-hungry leaders who destroy value and individuals with so much power and so little integrity that they can destroy our financial systems and then require us to rescue them.

Exploitation of the weak by the strong has become embedded into many of the corporate and business norms for success. Exploitation comes about when the Principles of Respect and Justice are ignored. Fraud, deceit and corruption follow when Truth and Respect are violated. The erosion of Trust in so many of our companies and institutions is an end result of the absence of the Humanity Principles in the processes and systems of those organisations. We have seen much more evidence of the antithesis to the Humanity Principles than their presence.

Corporations have the touchstone of the law, regulations and corporate governance requirements to use as their moral compass. Because the law does not provide morality, it only provides rules and statutes in the letter of the law, there can always be found loopholes and structures that enable corporations to get away with NOT taking responsibility; which individuals acting for them might feel constrained to take if applicable in their personal lives.

As I have already observed in the Chapter on Justice, the UK's Companies Act 2006 already requires its directors to promote the success of the company, by addressing the interests of its employees, fostering good business relationships with its suppliers and customers and by considering the impact of the company's operations on the community and the environment. For some company leaders, this has been sufficient direction to enable their modus operandi and activities to reflect the respect and fairness that is due to its employees and customers. Other leaders, (without empathy and consideration for the humane side of things) have sought the loop-holes and taken a cut-throat approach to business, cutting staff, cheating customers and squeezing suppliers under the imperative for profit.

Who therefore can be pointed to, that is already behaving in ways that I'm suggesting and is successful? For I have been told that it must undoubtedly be proven to those who use the profit measuring stick, that these suggestions work in practice; that as well as delivering humane interactions, that they will, as well, deliver profits.

Two organisations constituted very differently to the classic limited liability company, who have been practising a more humanely focused agenda over a long period of time, are The John Lewis Partnership and Arup. These organisations have been highly successful over many decades, from a business growth and profit perspective. Together, their examples strongly demonstrate how much more can be accomplished if a humane agenda is embedded deeply into the purpose, constitution and operational rules that make them work.

What Success Looks Like
The John Lewis Partnership

John Lewis has been in existence in some form for 150 years. It was in 1929 that John Spedan Lewis put his shares of ownership into Trust and established a Constitution with 7 Principles and a number of rules, by which the organisation was to function. There is even a body (called the Registry) which is empowered to ensure that the way the organisation is run is in harmony and integrity with the John Spedan Lewis vision and the Principles of the Constitution. The Principles state the purpose of the organisation and the principled guidelines upon which it would operate, including the ownership structure and standards of the relationships that the Partnership would have.

By all measures it has been a consistently growing and highly successful organisation. It is the UK's largest example of co-ownership and has 91,000 Partners. The Constitution of the Partnership provides for the democratic involvement of employees as co-owners of the business.

The first principle clearly states the "ultimate purpose is the happiness of all its members, through their worthwhile and satisfying employment in a successful business" granting them the responsibility of its ownership and its rewards also, unusually recognising these rewards as profit, knowledge and power. Partners are provided with extensive information and knowledge on all aspects of the business operations and are encouraged to take an active interest in promoting its commercial success.

The first principle empowers and acknowledges the Power that sits in every Partner.

There is an open, transparent and democratic process for every partner to engage in all aspects of the organisation and how it operates, enabling the Partners to use their Power to make the difference. There is not the wish for engagement of their employees that most organisations ask for but don't necessarily get, but there is a real engagement instead. There is a complete instituted communication and engagement system that operates up and down all layers of employees to ensure they know and contribute to the issues and decisions that the managers and leaders may want to take. There is a process for each Partner to make their views known and for their views to really influence the decision to be taken.

These processes don't happen once every six months, or even quarterly as some companies practice – this happens every week; via their Gazette, each Partner may express views or opinions or pose questions that will get answers from their leadership. One of their rules states: *"Information is the basis of democratic participation. The Partnership aims for openness, tolerance and freedom to express criticism, questions and suggestions (even at the risk of controversy)."* It doesn't allow its managers to suppress difference or conflict, as in some organisations I have experienced. Partners are strongly advised to perceive themselves as owners of the business and to respond in all scenarios as such, whether dealing with customers, suppliers or their local community. The responsibilities that go with that privilege are emphasised, encouraging them to consider other Partners today and in the future, for whom they are creating a legacy, by virtue of their decisions today.

This enables the Power of the Partners to be expressed in an excellent flow of communication of ideas, constructive suggestions and criticisms for the advancement of their business. Instead of 1% of an organisation's intelligence being applied to the challenges of the efficiency and growth of their business (the normal percentage of senior leaders in most organisations really addressing critical issues of change, growth and development) the John Lewis Partnership attempts to garner 100% of its organisational power, intelligence and creativity and put it to good use.

In their 2014 annual report they mention how a system developed in a call centre in Scotland was taken up by employees in other parts of the business to help them improve processes in their local business. This example demonstrates that good ideas can take root, and then transfer in an ecology and environment that is healthy. It remains healthy because such principles as integrity, respect, honesty, trust and fairness are practiced and thrive.

It remains healthy because the power of each individual is allowed to flow freely to make their contribution into their workplace and community. The community spirit thrives both inside the company as the Partners respect and are courteous with one another and it thrives as they deal with their customers and their suppliers with truth and honesty. They recognise that in order for themselves to do well, all parties in the transaction must do well.

I enjoy the atmosphere and environment of the John Lewis and Waitrose stores. They are unique in the sense that the Partners are the real owners of the stores and their reactions to any enquiries, or problems are the responses of an owner – not an employee. The environment feels different. Speaking to the assistants (partners) feels different – each person wants to help – to be useful, they want you to be happy as a result of your visit.

The John Lewis Partnership Constitution is very clear on their responsibility regarding their communities, suppliers and the environment, encouraging them to build relationships based on honesty, Respect and Trust, and these still actively guide how the organisation does its business. When the Partners engage with their suppliers they are interested to ensure that fair dealings and concern for that suppliers' future livelihood is taken into account through the transactions that they make. One of their rules states that *"The Partnership's relationships with its suppliers must be based, as with its customers, on honesty, fairness, courtesy and promptness. It looks for a similar attitude throughout its supply chains. In particular, the Partnership expects its suppliers to obey the law and to respect the wellbeing of their employees, their local communities and the environment."* Here Justice is expressed by fairness and Truth by honesty, Respect by courtesy and promptness.

The importance of the John Lewis Partnership model is that all organisations can learn how their structures and processes ensure real engagement by their partners. There is a true ownership for the experience of their customers, their suppliers' commitment and loyalty and true accountability of their leaders.

Accountability

The Constitution of the Partnership aims to ensure that the co-owners are given the information they need to be able to decide whether the Chairman, the Partnership Board and management are being effective. The Partnership's democratically elected bodies, including the Partnership Council and other elected councils and forum, provide regular opportunities at all levels of the business for management to report to Partners and for Partners to question management. This is very different from the one day a year when the Chairman and the Executive team report to its shareholders at the AGM. It is very different when leaders and managers hold their employees to account for their performance, but rarely reverse the situation to allow their employees to hold them to account for their performance. Here there is true equality, both at an individual level, but also in the ability to hold all parties to account for good conduct, courtesy, justice, fairness, honesty and good performance.

Traditional companies can learn from this example by instituting their own forum for employees to engage with, in which they can communicate, challenge and interact with their Executive team and layers of managers.

Performance and Rewards

The employee-owned model allows them to make capital investments in their business that will lead to long term benefits. In the year 2013/14 investment in Waitrose was £316.6m, up £118.4m (59.7%) on the previous year, and in John Lewis investment was £174.8m, up £30.5m (21.1%). They expect the higher level of capital investment to continue in 2014/15. By all economic metrics, the organisation has thrived at a time when most companies have shrunk.

The sales and productivity of each of its partners is measured with gross sales per average partner increasing from £161,700 in 2009-10 moving higher in each subsequent year, to £182,000 in the financial year 2013-14.

Partners share the rewards of their ownership, via a bonus which is paid every year from profits. Each partner receives the same percentage based on their basic salary. In 2013, the bonus was 17% of salary. In 2014, Partners shared £202.5m which represented 15% of pay. Everyone benefits equally. Additional benefits include Partner discounts, subsidised dining, leisure facilities, career development and a final salary non-contributory pension scheme.

Some of the greatest benefits that Partners receive as owners, is the lifestyle that goes with being a partner, including access to country houses for their holidays, yachts for the Yachting Club, and participation in Holiday Clubs which own a variety of venues that Partners and their families can enjoy; many other clubs and associations with equipment and venues, all such benefits being provided at extremely favourable rates that enable them to enjoy a quality of life that is beyond what their normal salary could afford them.

The remarkable experience I have when dealing with any John Lewis Partner, is the absence of fear. In comparison to many companies which I have worked with, or been present at, fear is present in a variety of ways and intensities in their people, whilst it is absent is John Lewis or Waitrose. People there are mostly happy, open, enthusiastic, supportive and helpful! As examples to illustrate the range of fear that can be generated by companies, these come to mind: employees of biotech and pharma companies fear animal rights activists and other protestors, employees of oil or mining companies fear accidents or death, and employees of many generic companies fear their managers and/or suffer the threat of not achieving the required standards of performance and being fired. Fear as a quality is not nice to have if you're the person expressing it – it's damaging to your mind and emotions and it's not easy to experience when you're at the other end receiving it, if you're the customer, coach or supplier. Fear restricts performance and ease of accomplishment.

In the John Lewis Partnership there is an enforced equality written into the principles and rules of the organisation, though pay scales reflect the different levels and responsibilities of Partners. The rules determine that the pay differential between the highest paid Partner will be no more than 75 times the average basic pay of non-management Partners. That may appear to be a great deal, but it's approximately half of the average FTSE 100 Company, whose CEO's average pay is 145 times greater.

Financial Performance

In their Annual Report for 2013-14 the Partnership confirmed that both Waitrose and John Lewis increased market share for the fifth consecutive year, profit before exceptionals grew by almost 10% and sales grew 6.6% on top of 2013's sales of £9.5bn to £10.2 bn. This was the first time they achieved sales of over £10 billion, putting them on a par with the turnover of Marks & Spencer – around 43rd place of the FTSE 100 (had they been quoted).

Both Waitrose and John Lewis grew sales well ahead of their respective markets, increasing their market share. Waitrose outperformed the Kantar Grocery Market by 5.8% and John Lewis outperformed the BRC Retail Index by 4.3%. Their Return on Capital Employed (ROIC is a useful metric to assess the long-term value creation of a business) has increased year on year between 7.2% and 8.5% for the last five years. During 2014, the Partnership created 6,300 net new jobs, thereby making another constructive contribution to employment in Britain.

By any standard of financial and performance evaluation the John Lewis Partnership has achieved growth and profits over a period of time where most organisations have struggled and most especially in the retail space. Their forward strategy remains focused on their ultimate goal — balancing the happiness of the Partners with the success of the business as a whole.

What Success Looks Like At Arup

Arup (officially Arup Group Limited) was founded in 1946 by Ove Arup, with an initial focus on structural engineering, but over the years has expanded to include designers, engineers of all kinds, planners, consultants and technical specialists for delivering most things in the built environment. It is a multinational professional services firm headquartered in London, UK with over 91 offices across Europe, the Americas, Africa, Australasia and South East Asia with 12,000 employees.

Ove Arup and The Key Speech

Arup was originally a partnership, but was later established as a trust owned for its employees and dependants by philosopher and engineer Ove Arup. He outlined the key business principles of the organisation in a 'key speech' in 1970 and the principles he detailed there have become the touchstone of guidance and focus for different leaders and Boards over the years.

In the Key Speech, Ove Arup identified the first aim of work is that it be interesting and rewarding. He details that projects should be focused on quality, with fitness for purpose, satisfying or significant forms and economy of construction. He names this focus 'Total Architecture' and says that as human beings *"we need the stimulation produced by excellence."*

He identified the second purpose of the organisation as each human being's right to pursue happiness, with the requirement for each person to accept moral and humanitarian restraints. The humanitarian attitude he explains means seeing every member *"as a human being whose happiness is the concern of all, who is treated not only as a means but as an end."* He advocates that the humanitarian attitude should be extended to all 'collaborators' both inside the organisation and outside. He recognises the importance of making the environment and working conditions as pleasant as possible. He strongly advocates acting *'honourably in our dealings with our own and other people' and emphasises justifying 'the trust of our clients by giving their interest first priority in the work we do for them'*. He recognises the need for fairness and equality, avoiding discrimination and nepotism. His humanitarianism acknowledges a social conscience with a wish to do 'socially useful work and to join hands with others fighting for the same values'.

His third aim was *'prosperity for all our members'* and says *"Most people would say that is our main aim, this is why we are in business. But it would be wrong to look at it as our main aim. We should look at it as an essential prerequisite for even the partial fulfilment of any of our aims. For it is an aim which, if over-emphasised, easily gets out of hand and becomes very dangerous for our harmony, unity and very existence."*

The value of these statements is that they define the vision and priorities of a humanitarian organisation in a clear, focused way that cannot be misconstrued by future leaders. The first priority places people's desire to produce excellence as the prime driver of the organisation's existence and secondly to produce happiness for its people, with all the attending humanity principles to ensure their happiness. Thirdly he recognises financial success as an aim, with warnings of its ability to destroy harmony and unity, if it is over-emphasised and gets out of hand.

Arup Ownership Structure

Arup's ownership structure ensures that it retains an independent spirit, while holding the firm accountable to its own people for its social and corporate responsibility. With no external shareholders (the trusts own the shares) or external investors, the leaders of the firm are able to determine the firm's priorities and direction. The business is made up of people who share a strongly aligned set of values which have been at the core of their activities since the firm was founded.

In respect of governance, the capital of Arup Group Limited is divided into equity shares, which are held in trust for the benefit of the employees (past and present) of the Arup group of companies, whilst voting shares are held by the Ove Arup Partnership Charitable Trust. Arup policy is set by its Group Board, which in turn reports to the firm's Trustees, who include representatives of the global college of directors and principals who are active in the business.

Employee involvement in the Group's performance is encouraged and maintained via participation in a staff profit sharing initiative. Each of Arup's employees receives a share of the firm's operating profit each year, though not an equal percentage based on salary as at the John Lewis Partnership.

Leadership and Democracy at Arup

The Arup organisation doesn't benefit from a democratic, structured involvement of all its employees from their initial employment to post employment. Hence the personal sense of ownership of the organisation sometimes appears to be missing at the lower levels of the organisation; though in my personal experience, there is a fierce loyalty to the culture and the opportunities that it provides to its employees for personal growth, satisfaction and service.

Arup's strategy is to attract the best and brightest people and then develop their skills so that the organisation can deliver the best projects for their clients and stakeholders. They make a strong commitment to career progression for all their people through continuous professional development and the Arup University programmes.

The Group is active with regular employee communications and employees are encouraged to express their views on major policy issues. 'Working at Arup' surveys are conducted to obtain feedback from employees. This survey is confidential and is used alongside consultation with employees where appropriate. Each year, employees are provided with a Chairman's report and financial information. Employees are informed of significant business issues via the use of email, discussions with senior management, the Group's intranet and in-house publications.

Arup commits to a sustainable approach in all its projects through a formal sustainability policy which is embraced by the individuals that together make up the firm. These shared values (quality, sustainability, diversity, honourable dealings and service) unify Arup people, because they are not values just espoused. They are values and principles that have been practised consistently for over half a century. In 2014, for the fourth consecutive year, Arup was named in "The Times Top 50 Employers for Women", formally recognising the firm as one of the top 50 companies in the UK to lead the way in gender equality in the workplace.

Arup Business Results

The Arup organisation has tripled in size in the last ten years, and now numbers over 12,000 people worldwide. The financial report for the 12 months to 31 March 2013 confirmed that the firm surpassed £1 billion in turnover for the first time in Arup's history, while operating profits remained positive at £23.7m. In their announced results for 2013, the Group turnover for the year increased by 3.9% (2012: 2.6%) and the Group made a total profit before tax, dividends and staff profit share of £56m.

Turnover and profit per person is a financial KPI (Key Performance Indicator) used to monitor the continued contribution to the Group. In calculating this measure, profit is stated before tax, dividends and staff profit share. For the year ended 31 March 2013, Group turnover per person was £95k (2012: £98k) and profit per person was £5k (2012: £6k).

The following two quotes emphasise the importance of employees' vital contribution to the success of their companies: "Employee-owned companies currently contribute some £25 billion to the British economy. According to an annual index compiled by a leading law firm, they outperform the FTSE by roughly 10% each year." The Guardian, Tuesday 16 March 2010. "Studies have shown that employee-owned businesses generally outperform non-employee-owned businesses where employees do not have a significant stake in ownership or the right to participate in decision-making." Cass Business School, January 2010. *This is strong evidence for shareholders to strongly consider revising the salary and benefits currently provided to the executive team and require a more equal distribution of such benefits, just to ensure better performance.*

Arup and the John Lewis Partnership both allow for ownership by staff, inclusion and reward that directly compensates employees for their commitment and performance. Both were begun with humanitarian objectives, which have consistently been met, delivering successful results for employees and customers for more than half a century.

SUMMARY REFLECTIONS

The examples provided by the John Lewis Partnership and Arup demonstrate that a single leader with a vision can change an organisation in their lifetime in ways that have effects well beyond their own lifetime. Their vision and the human principles that they caused to be practised have changed the lives of thousands of people employed by their organisation and millions of customers who have benefited from them.

The principles that they and those that followed them have translated into activities and systems have ensured a continuance of principles before profits, yet paradoxically have caused thriving financial returns. They have created pleasurable experiences for their customers and respect and security for their suppliers; they have benefited the community and environments in which they have operated. They have left a legacy to the beneficiaries of the principles they held dear.

Their demonstration at one level appears moderate, humble even, not at all enlightened or spiritual. Yet their examples have been to assure us that putting humanity first, people before profits can and does lead to better results for all. They have made work meaningful to those employed by the organisation and purposeful to those of us who benefit from their work; in the beautiful functional buildings engineered by Arup and in trustworthy, retail experiences that enhance our everyday lives in the case of John Lewis.

Arup and the John Lewis Partnership are only two examples of which there more organisations recognising the need to change and adopt more democratic, human principled structures that facilitate meaningful work to benefit employees, customers and stakeholders. In early 2015, a UK accounting firm – Grant Thornton – announced an employee consultation to create a shared enterprise model that would allow all 4,500 of its people to have a say and stake in the firm. Their avowed intent is to create an environment in which everyone will think and act like an owner.

There are and will be many others – not exactly the same in structure – but motivated by the same recognition that as humans we need to aspire to more, to be more, as well as do more.

Not all organisations need to operate an ownership structure for success. All the ingredients of success, the open inclusion of employees, sharing responsibilities and rewards, and many other aspects suggested previously, could certainly be replicated. The ownership structures were the easiest form of organisation to ensure that those human principles were applied, but not necessarily the only form. The important point is that these organisations began with a set of human principles that played out in the vision and the practises that enabled them to bring those principles alive.

Their example shows us that alignments to human principles when implemented into a corporate organisation can have manifold beneficial impacts. They help leaders today see that acts of enlightenment are not that far away from what they can conceive. In the words of Napolean Hill, *"Whatever your mind can conceive and believe the mind can achieve"*.

CONCLUSION

The book began with a catalogue of problems that big business has created by its ruthless focus to deliver 'value to shareholders' forgetting that business is actually delivered by human beings, for human beings and within communities of human beings. It highlighted many instances of corporate malpractice and suggested the global financial meltdown caused by banks and financial institutions were caused by an absence of fundamental human principles of Truth, Respect, Justice, Integrity and Trust. It detailed the damage that the absence of these principles has had on the psyche and wellbeing of people individually and the impact these toxic practices have had in perpetrating deceit, fraud and corruption on the many.

The book makes the case that doctors have an ethos that controls their practise of medicine to 'Do no harm' and business should also set itself standards of a similar nature. As a base level to do no harm, and then to do what it has the power to do, to do extreme good in the world. Business systems have a power of their own, that can fundamentally alter personal behaviours. The Humanity Principles give us access to our own power to not succumb to lower standards than our own and to not only exist successfully in any organisation, but even to change it for the better.

Human beings have an evolving consciousness that is growing and changing to perceive better truths and to act more ethically, so that people can improve their physical, mental and emotional well-being. This evolving consciousness is combining with the recognition that how big business is currently operating is problematic and needs to change to have better governance, better standards and ethics and higher forms of contracts and engagements between employees and their companies.

As humans, we have innate power to do good when we allow the promptings of the Humanity Principles. Truth, Respect, Fairness/Justice, Integrity and Trust are inner mind-sets that can be grown to allow us to perceive more deeply and to behave more humanely. All of them are innate programmes that run naturally in individuals, but having them run in business is more challenging, but can be more rewarding as organisations have enhanced power through the collective gathering of people and resources that can then be applied to positive outcomes. The question is asked how these principles can become active components in more businesses so that they benefit employees, suppliers and people globally.

Each principle was examined to extract new clarities and perceptions of its constitution and how and where it can be applied, as well as clues to identify its absence or abuse. Examples of how the principles can be practised are also provided, and the point is made, that they need to become active in the thinking and action of people in work. When organisations misbehave, they lose peoples' custom as well as their trust. These are punishments that people will exact when businesses do not adhere to these basic human principles. There is an additional point made – that in our evolving world, the traditional big, hierarchical business may become obsolete if people refuse to work for it, or choose not to buy its products. In particular, the younger generation require work that is more purposeful and meaningful, and a pay cheque at the end of the month will not be sufficient to retain them.

Such messages are a warning to companies choosing to continue on this inhumane trajectory and are an encouragement to take a different fork in the road, to realign to principles that anchor their organisation to serve more people than just a select few. Examples of both big and small companies are given, with good and bad outcomes that naturally arise from choices made.

Ultimately, my message is one of hope. The human principles I have detailed are already programmed into us. They operate naturally, when we don't swamp them with unnatural programmes of competition, greed, deceit and fraud. If we allow humane feelings to come into play in our work contexts, to allow empathy to operate, to see that the person we are negotiating with also needs to win, as well as ourselves, we can create meaningful exchanges and valuable relationships that make our working lives rich with purpose and meaning. We can create environments that heal people and do not harm them. We can create contexts in which individuals can contribute their talents and strengths to make a positive difference to other people and our world.

The work and the resultant rewards of the humanity principled approach is still a work in progress. Will the work ever end? I hope not! It can and should be at the heart of our evolving and growing human consciousness and therefore at the heart of our progressive business consciousness.

APPENDIX I

The Principles of the John Lewis Partnership

Principle 1 — **Purpose**

The Partnership's ultimate purpose is the happiness of all its members, through their worthwhile and satisfying employment in a successful business. Because the Partnership is owned in trust for its members, they share the responsibilities of ownership, as well as its rewards – profit, knowledge and power."

Principle 2 — **Power**

Power in the Partnership is shared between three governing authorities, the Partnership Council, the Partnership Board and the Chairman.

Principle 3 — **Profit**

The Partnership aims to make sufficient profit from its trading operations to sustain its commercial vitality, to finance its continued development, to distribute a share of those profits each year to its members, and to enable it to undertake other activities consistent with its ultimate principles

Principle 4 — **Members**

The Partnership aims to employ and retain as its members people of ability and integrity who are committed to working together and to supporting its Principles. Relationships are based on mutual respect and courtesy with as much equality between its members as differences or responsibility permit. The

Partnership aims to recognise their individual contributions and reward them fairly."

Principle 4 evokes the principle of respect and integrity as the measures of who is to be employed by the Partnership. It lays out the importance of such standards to bring the commitment and support of its membership.

Principle 5 — **Customers**

The Partnership aims to deal honestly with its customers and secure their loyalty and trust by providing outstanding choice, value and service."

Principle 5 advocates the embodiment of truth and honesty in the service provision with its customers.

Principle 6 — **Business Relationships**

The Partnership aims to conduct all its business relationships with integrity and courtesy and scrupulously to honour every business agreement."

Principle 6 confirms the importance of integrity in all business relationships, contracts and supply chain.

Principle 7 — **The Community**

The Partnership aims to obey the spirit as well as the letter of the law and to contribute to the well-being of the communities where it operates.

Principle 7 confirms the alignment to justice within the domain of the partnership and asks that it contribute this justice and fairness into the communities in which it operates.

APPENDIX II

The United Nations Global Compact

A base standard has been set by the United Nations in its Global Compact as it asks for organisations to sign up to their 10 Principles.

Their first focus on Human Right states;

Principle 1 — Businesses should support and respect the protection of internationally proclaimed human rights; and

Principle 2 — make sure that they are not complicit in human rights abuses.

Their secondary focus on Labour asks that;

Principle 3 — Businesses should uphold the freedom of association and the effective recognition of the right to collective bargaining;

Principle 4 — the elimination of all forms of forced and compulsory labour;

Principle 5 — the effective abolition of child labour; and

Principle 6 — the elimination of discrimination in respect of employment and occupation.

Principle 7 — Businesses should support a precautionary approach to environmental challenges;

Principle 8 — undertake initiatives to promote greater environmental responsibility; and

Principle 9 — encourage the development and diffusion of environmentally friendly technologies.

Principle 10 — Businesses should work against corruption in all its forms, including extortion and bribery.

REFERENCES

Michael J. Sandel, *What Money Can't Buy* published by Penguin, 2012.

Iain Martin, * *Making It Happen: Fred Goodwin, RBS and The Men Who Blew Up the British Economy* published Simon & Shuster UK, 2013.

Robert Weissman, *What The List Tells Us*, Editor, Multinational Monitor published online.

Matt Taibbi, *Gangster Bankers: Too Big to Jail* article published online

Ha-Joon Chang, *23 Things They Don't Tell You About Capitalism,* published by Penguin 2010.

Tony Hsieh, *Delivering Happiness*, CEO of Zappos.com, Inc. published by Business Plus, 2010.

Joseph E. Stiglitz, *The Price of Inequality,* published by Penguin 2013.

Professor Clive Boddy, *Corporate Psychopaths: Organisational Destroyers*, papers for Middlesex University.

Abraham Maslow, A Theory of Human Motivation, in Psychological Review -1943 paper. And **A.H. Maslow**, *Critique of Self-Actualization Theory*, in: **E. Hoffman (Ed.)**, *Future visions: The Unpublished Papers of Abraham Maslow* published by Thousand Oaks, CA: Sage, 1996.

The Most Dangerous Man in America — a documentary on the release of the Pentagon Papers by **Daniel Ellensberg**, released 11 Sep 2009.

Sissella Bok, *Common Values,* book published August 5, 2002

Companies Act 2006 (UK).
www.legislation.gov.uk/ukpga/2006/46/contents

The Arbinger Institute, *Leadership and Self Deception*, published by Penguin January 5, 2010.

The Corporation is a 2003 Canadian documentary **film** written by University of British Columbia law professor **Joel Bakan**, and directed by **Mark Achbar** and **Jennifer Abbott**.

Ray Anderson, CEO of Interface Inc in the movie *The Corporation**.

John Rawls, *A Theory of Justice*, published by Oxford Paperbacks, 1971.

Mark Carney, Governor of the Bank of England, 2014 speech in London.

The United Nations Global Compact
www.unglobalcompact.org

Napolean Hill, *Whatever Your Mind Can Conceive And Believe the Mind Can Achieve*.

Marc Barry, *Competitive Intelligence Professional**.

Adam Smith, *Causes of The Wealth of Nations,* published in 1776.

Professor John Whitney of Columbia Business School, *Taking Charge: Management Guide for Troubled Companies and Turnarounds* paper published 1986.

Carl Jung, *Psychological Types*. Princeton University Press, 1971. *The Significance of Constitution and Heredity in Psychology* (November 1929).

Stephen R. Covey, *Principle Centred Leadership*, published by Simon & Shuster, 1990.

Mahatma Gandhi, *The Story Of My Experiments With Truth*, re-published 2014.

Mitch Feierstein, *Planet Ponzi; How The World Got Into This Mess, What Happens Next, How to Save Yourself*, published by Bantam Books, 2012.

Jonathan Haidt, *The Righteous Mind* published by Penguin 2012

Tertullian, *Apologeticus.*

William Wordsworth, *The Prelude* written 1805.

Made in Dagenham, film released 2010, directed by **Nigel Cole**.

Brian J. Robertson, *Holacracy: The Revolutionary Management System That Abolishes Hierarchy* Paperback– 4 Jun 2011.

ABOUT THE AUTHOR

Penny is the founder and Managing Director of Corporate Alchemy Limited, a people development company providing executive coaching and training to executives and managers of FTSE 100 companies, multi-national and professional services organisations. Personally, she has worked one to one with more than a thousand senior executives from 75 different organisations. Since 2003, she has led a team of coaches, trainers and psychometric consultants, delivering personal development programmes on the inter-personal and humane skills that build leadership effectiveness, confidence, capability and healthy environments.

Penny has worked with Board level executives, directors and managers in multi- national companies, engineering consultants, lawyers and accountants solving personal, systemic, cultural and process problems affecting their business. She is a trusted adviser to many leaders who use her services repeatedly, for themselves and their teams. Her unique humane approach has helped businesses grow their people and their business by an average 30% during the time of her assistance, both in terms of people and new income.

She has also worked with small and medium sized businesses between 1999 and 2002, providing management consultancy services.

Earlier in her career, Penny worked in the City of London financial services industry, working for international banks, including Chase Manhattan, as a marketing specialist in investment banking, providing a range of capital market products and services. She worked closely with CEOS and CFO's worldwide, helping them raise finance in the Euromarkets. Her roles involved international travel (to over 32 countries) giving talks, presentations and seminars as part of the sales and marketing activities. She also worked at the London Stock Exchange, as Listing Manager in the Capital Markets Group. So she has experienced first-hand the thinking, attitudes and alignments of multi-national corporate organisations and experienced directly the nature of people and systems in financial services firms.

Penny professionally re-trained as a business coach in 2002 and became accredited with the ICF as a

Professional Certified Coach. Her other business credentials include being a Fellow of the Institute of Leadership and Management and a member of the Institute of Directors since 2000.